PRAISE FOR THE GIRL WHO WALKED IN THE SHADOW OF THE KING

"I loved this story. What drew me page after page was Shelly's ability to give us a peek into the unseen Kingdom realm where God is fighting for us—and what she shows us is wonderful and powerful. The tenacity of God's redemptive plans for each of us is unrelenting. He never 'writes us off.' Even when we don't see it, He is there, continuing to pursue us for the purpose of redeeming and healing us. Shelly's story will inspire women at any point in their journeys toward truth and freedom, whether they are seekers, new believers, or seasoned women of faith dealing with brokenness in their own lives."

Shery Miller
Director of the Women's Ministry Leadership Team
Springs Church, Colorado Springs

"Shelly's is a powerful story of redemption and restoration. I've personally walked with her over two decades as she's not only experienced victory in her own life, but empowered others to do the same. As a pastor, I've told Shelly's story countless times in ministering to men and women choosing to lay hold of freedom in Christ, and I know that her story in print will impact even more lives. As Shelly's life so beautifully illustrates, there is freedom and healing in Christ—for all of us."

Pastor Steve Collins
Founding Pastor, Church Eleven 32

"I absolutely love Shelly's imagery of God's presence, His thoughts, and His pursuit of our hearts even when life hurts. I'm reminded of the beloved poem 'Footprints in the Sand' that has resonated with folks for years. Shelly's story elaborates on that idea by giving us a glimpse of how God loves and carries us no matter what our circumstances, even if we have yet to recognize that He has been there all along."

Shellie Rushing Tomlinson
Author, Speaker, and Podcast Host of All Things Southern

"The names of God reveal so much about who He is, and one of the things that resonated with me about Shelly's story is that it so beautifully reflects this truth. Shelly paints beautiful portraits that showcase the names and facets of God. When we come into the presence of the Lord, acknowledging all that He is—Savior, Protector, Shepherd, King—our time with Him is enriched in every way. Shelly has experienced this in her life, and we can too."

Gaylyn Williams
President of Relationship Resources and Author of 2031 Names of God

"I've never read a book with such fascination, wondering how God was going to work in, and speak into, the life of its author. If you need encouragement that God is always there, I'd encourage you to seek Him with your whole heart, as Shelly does, and you'll hear His still, small voice whispering to you, too."

Eric Elder
Author of St. Nicholas: The Believer

The GIRL WHO WALKED IN THE SHADOW *of* THE KING

FINDING GOD *in the* JOURNEY

SHELLY BUSBY

ILLUMIFY MEDIA GLOBAL
Littleton, Colorado

Published by Illumify Media Global

www.IllumifyMedia.com

Library of Congress Control Number:

Paperback ISBN: 978-1546988-07-6

eBook ISBN: 978-1-949021-32-5

Dedicated to Jesus in whose shadow I continue...

Now to the King eternal, immortal, invisible, the only God, be honor and glory forever and ever. Amen.

(1 Timothy 1:17)

I sought the Lord, and He answered me;
He delivered me from all my fears.
Those who look to Him are radiant;
their faces are never covered with shame.
(Psalm 34:4-5)

CONTENTS

FOREWORD

Where were you, God?

If you've ever felt traumatized by life, perhaps you've asked this question. And if you're still hurting, you might be asking that question now: *God, where are you?*

Shelly Busby provides an answer in her inspiring story of God's redemptive power at work in a real-life, beautiful, messy family.

The first time I read her story, not only was I moved to tears, I also found myself thinking about the "characters" in her story for days. Going about my daily tasks, I'd catch myself reflecting on their journeys, pondering over the mysteries and miracles of all that eventually transpired in each of their lives.

I use the word "characters" loosely, of course, because these are not fictional people, but very real hearts and souls, and I found myself falling in love with every one of them.

How could I not when Shelly paints such a vibrant portrait of a flawed, hurting family caught in the crosshairs of God's restorative power and stubborn love?

How Shelly sees God in her story, how she sees God's heart towards others in her story, and how she sees His redemptive design in every chapter of her story will change forever how you view events, people, and experiences in your own life.

Shelly's perspective may be fresh and relevant, but the pain she describes comes from temptations and failings as old as time itself: Rebellion. Abuse. Divorce. Shame. Insecurities. Selfishness. Addictions. Obsessions. Shelly's life has been shaped by all of these and more. And yet none of these have had the last word in her story.

And they don't have to have the last word in our stories, either.

Have you ever asked:

Does God see what I'm going through? Does He even care?

Can there be healing and restoration in my family?

I long for so much more—isn't there more than this?

Can my life ever feel whole or beautiful again?

If so, the pages you hold in your hands will speak to your heart. And the answer, as you are about to find out, is a resounding and beautiful yes.

Karen Linamen Bouchard

Author of Just Hand Over the Chocolate and No One Will Get Hurt

ACKNOWLEDGMENTS

I would like to thank a few of the precious people who have played a role in my living—and telling—this story:

My husband, Brad—My love, the journey is better because we walk it together.

My children, Jake, Jessie, and Anna—God continues to reveal Himself to me through you. May you always see God in your journey.

Mom, thank you for encouraging me to press on; even when it cost you deeply. Thank you for loving me when I was unlovable and for never giving up on me.

Dad, thank you for being my first glimpses of Jesus. I love you more than you can know.

Miss Ellie, thank you for giving me a special place in your heart. I know I'm always welcome there.

Ben, Jenny, and Chris I love you with all my heart.

Pastor Steve and Lisa Collins, thanks for taking us in, calling us your own and providing a place in which to grow.

Eric Elder, this story would not be written if it weren't for you. Thank you for countless hours spurring and encouraging me to "march forth"!

Karen Bouchard, thank you for believing in me and this book. Your friendship is a priceless jewel.

I am surrounded by a sea of friends and family who have helped shape my life and my family for eternity. I am continuously thankful for you. And to my other sisters Kathy Snowden, Sue Cohen, my Miss Toni, Donna Petty, Donna Kent, Jinko Liebold, Kit Willock, Krista Goodin, Deb Brinlee, Sarah Troublefield, and Graciela Powell, Heaven calls!

PROLOGUE

*E*very person has a story. Some of the chapters are filled with treasure, others with pain.

As I began to write down the events of my story, I asked the Lord to help me string my memories together in a meaningful way. As the memories spilled onto the pages, something unexpected happened: I began to see these events—the good, bad, and ugly—from God's perspective. In fact, it was as if I could see my whole life from His viewpoint, as best as I could perceive it.

Imagine seeing your life through the eyes of God the King!

I am not a theologian, and this is not a theological book. My hope is to share my story to testify to the goodness of Christ Jesus. In writing out my own story, I have become convinced that God's presence in our lives *has* always been—and *is* always—there. Best of all, the more time we spend seeking the face of God, listening for and to His voice, the more we find evidence of Him *everywhere*.

There are tough truths and challenging experiences related to my family in these pages. I share these to shed light on the bigger truth that, despite our iniquity and shortcomings, God's grace, goodness, and redemptive power surpass any challenge we face. The dark and ugly seasons of my story have since been redeemed by Jesus Christ.

You will see, reflected in my childhood memories, the presence of the King Himself, although I was not aware of Him at the time. Eventually, I learned His name and was taught about Him, but He seemed invisible and distant. I couldn't hear or perceive Him in any practical way. He was just some famous third party—an unseen Presence. I knew *of* Him, but I didn't know *Him*.

And yet He knew me. He followed me everywhere—like a shadow; quiet and mostly unrealized.

I did not turn to fully meet Him until many years later. It would be decades before I recognized the evidence and impact of His presence through my whole life.

My hope is that this story will stir in you an awareness of His presence in your own life—even if and when you haven't sensed Him there. You are not invisible to Him, *and you never have been*. He sees you. Embracing this truth—and understanding the loving, protective, redemptive way He sees you—will transform your story and your life. Are you ready for beautiful memories to be made even richer? Are you willing for painful memories to be redeemed and to discover meaning and treasure waiting for you even there?

May seeing Jesus in my story empower you to see Him ever more clearly in your own.

A JOURNEY BEGINS

Some of my best childhood memories are of being with my dad. My earliest recollection goes back to the winter of 1968. We lived in High Ridge, Missouri, about twenty miles southwest of St. Louis.

Though Mom and Dad grew up in the city, they loved the outdoors. Dad always had to be outside fishing, hiking, hunting, or camping. Once they'd saved enough money for a down payment on a house, they went rural and bought a house nestled on a wooded hill just up from a little lake.

I had just turned two-years-old that December when the lake froze. Mom bundled me in warm clothes. She helped with the stubborn zipper on my coat. "This thing! I need to fix it," she said, looking at me and smiling. She worked my stubby little fingers into fuzzy mittens and wrapped me in a yellow scarf. Great Grandma Rumpendihl had knitted the scarf just before she passed months earlier. It was made of wool and helped me remember her.

Dad grinned at me as he buttoned his coat. "Well . . . hmmff! Look at you. You're ready for a blizzard, aren't you?"

I smiled despite having no idea what he was talking about. What was a blizzard? I was proud that Dad was taking me out on a special adventure. Mom pulled the hood over my head and tucked the scarf inside.

We stepped out into the cold morning air. "Bye, Pepper!" I called, waving goodbye to my dog. Smoke billowed out the chimney as I looked back at Pepper wagging his tail. Dad unlatched the gate and led the way out.

It was a short walk down the hill to the lake. That day, the gravel road was hidden beneath a thick layer of soft snow. It was a cold winter, and another storm had blown through the night before, painting the scene white. That morning, the sun shone bright, bouncing rays off the glistening snow.

As we neared the lake, I extended my arms wide, slowly stretching forward, then to the sides, as if I could touch it all at once. It was spectacular. We made our way down the crunchy, snowy path. At the lake, Dad stood with one foot on the snow, the other on lake ice. "Here," he said, extending his arms toward mine.

We stood together at the edge of the frozen shore. I was both excited and frightened as my legs shook. I'd seen our black lab, Pepper, romp in the shallow waters of the lake numerous times that summer. The concept of a lake of ice didn't make sense. *Walk on water?*

Slowly, I reached my mitten-clad fingers to clutch Dad's strong grip. Dad stepped backward onto the lake. "You're okay, Shelly; just hold on. Pretend we're skating."

With hard ice beneath my feet and cold air on my cheeks, I looked around the lake. White surrounded us. It was beautiful. Snow covered the banks, and trees skirted the lake, heavy with a fresh blanket of white. The thrill of being on the ice sent shivers through my bundled limbs as I inhaled the cool air.

I could see Dad's breath as he beckoned me to step with him. "Come on. I've got you." I held tight as we moved. It was slick, like our kitchen floor after Mom mopped it and I would "skate" and slide in socks, amusing myself while Mom prepared dinner.

That was the first of many adventures. Dad was always stretching me to go where I wouldn't have gone on my own. He led, I followed. It might be scary, but Dad always talked me through it, patiently waiting for me to "step out." I was confident because I knew Dad was always there for me.

It was worth it every time. Dad's adventurous heart and gentle ways challenged and shaped me to face trials with courage. He taught me to keep a loose grip on the familiar and a ready hand open to grasp something new.

The King looked around the scene, admiring His work. Through the shimmer of light playing off the snow, He watched. The snowflakes pleased Him. Like His children, each bore His own remarkable beauty, perfected in uniqueness.

He watched the child. He watched the father. He watched their steps on the ice. He watched the neighbor collecting logs to burn on that cold, sunny winter day. He was there in the kitchen with the mother scrambling eggs in the pan, and He heard the dog whine at the gate, aching to frolic with its master. His eyes rested again on the girl engulfed in yellow. "Courage," He said to Himself. "The girl will learn to grow in courage."

Later that winter Dad caught a severe case of pneumonia, landing him in the hospital for a week. The cold winter months took a toll on him every year, and this time the doctor urged him to take a break from the cold, moist air. "Take a vacation. Go somewhere dry. You might even consider moving somewhere with a drier climate." Mom was six months pregnant when they loaded the car and went to Arizona for several weeks to dry out Dad's lungs. This was the first time either of them had been west of Missouri.

They fell in love with the mountains, mesas, and rugged terrain of the desert. It was different from the familiar rolling hills and thick woods of the Ozarks, but at least it offered adventure and dry air. It was a good fit. They could see themselves setting down roots in Arizona.

Back from their trip, they were excited to tell friends and family about their plans to move to Arizona and make the desert their home. Mom seemed ready for something new, and Dad talked about it all the time.

In early summer, Mom gave birth to my brother, Ben. Friends came over to help, celebrate, and dote on the new arrival. Dad still was talking about Arizona.

One weekend, late in fall, the trees were flush with rich hues of gold and crimson. Mom and Dad were barbecuing with friends. Dad started in on his talk about Arizona.

"You guys, the camping there . . ." He continued bragging until his childhood buddy, Rick, interrupted him.

"You know, Roger, you sure talk a lot about going to Arizona, but I don't see you doing anything about it."

Everyone chuckled, and then it got awkwardly quiet. These were good friends. They cared about one another and knew how sick Dad had been that year.

"Winter's coming," Rick pressed. "You really gonna make it here another year?"

Dad changed the subject, directing everyone's attention to the hot grilled brats and pork loin. "Look! Perfection again. Who's hungry?"

The next day, Dad loaded his pickup with his tools, our dog Pepper, and a suitcase. He told Mom he'd be back in two weeks. "I'm goin' to find work," he said, looking at her reassuringly. "Just two weeks."

He took Ben from Mom's arms and kissed his forehead, then turned to me. "Need you to be a good girl, Shell. Help Mom with Ben, okay?" He bent down and kissed my cheek.

We followed Dad out to the driveway and stood stunned as we watched him pull onto the gravel road, headed to Arizona.

Phoenix was coming into its own at that time. Real estate was booming, property was cheap, and work was easy to come by. Within a week Dad had landed a job as a journeyman plumber. He stayed an extra day, scouting out the new subdivisions of stucco homes springing up all over the valley. He found a house on the outskirts of Phoenix, phoned Mom, and said, "Call Rick and Laurie. I know they'll help. Time to pack everything up, Merry. We're moving to Arizona."

The next week, Mom and Dad put the High Ridge house up for lease and packed the truck, the wood-paneled station wagon, and a little U-Haul. Mom tucked fresh bottles of formula in the diaper bag for Ben before they said a final goodbye to friends and family and we set out on our new adventure.

The Shepherd kept watch as the little family packed their cars and the rented trailer, their unanswered questions and optimism visible to Him alone. As they exchanged long hugs with friends they were leaving behind, He surveyed the road ahead of them. Then He set loose a host of escorts to guard and guide them on their journey.

He weighed their doubts and fears, pleased that their hope and vision was hearty.

"They are full of excitement and anticipation—as they should be. They don't know how hard it will be after the newness wears off, but if they watch and listen, they will find new treasures I've prepared for them.

"In their loneliness I will be revealed.

"In their confusion I will reveal order.

"In their doubts I will confirm My will.
"In their surrender I will draw them close."

Dad hadn't wanted to leave behind our lab, but Pepper was accustomed to freely roaming the open acres of High Ridge. Before we left Missouri, Dad gifted him to our neighbor.

We quickly settled in. Mom personalized the pretty little Spanish-style house and made it our home. Dad had solid, steady work, and his health thrived in the clean, dry air. Each day promised clear blue skies. Mom would put Ben in the stroller, so we could take walks around our new neighborhood. The sunshine was bright, and it felt good on my skin. Something was missing though. We all missed Pepper. We were used to having a tail wagging beside us at every turn.

Before long we had another pup tagging along, though Bambi probably never really looked like a pup. A full-blooded Great Dane, she stood a head above me. I was around four years old by then, and she was my best friend—at least until other kids moved into the neighborhood. When I looked straight at her, I saw her long legs. They looked like dancing trees as she pranced.

Every afternoon, Bambi stretched her colt-like legs, running laps around the yard. For all her size, she was a gentle, willing playmate.

One afternoon, Bambi and I were running around out back. I imagined I was a pony galloping beside her. We ran round and round the little yard. "C'mon, Bambi," I called to her. "Let's go!" It was a fun game trying to keep up with her.

Suddenly there was a loud crash. The next-door neighbor, taking out trash in the alley, had accidentally tipped over a stainless-steel trash bin.

Startled, Bambi did an about-face and stopped dead in her tracks, her head turned and ears raised in alert.

I'd been running behind Bambi, and I couldn't stop. The next thing

I knew, I ran straight into Bambi's massive chest. Bambi's solid frame, eighty pounds greater than my own, met mine like a brick wall and sent me flying to a crushing fall, breaking my collarbone. She seldom barked, but in protective mode her windpipes were deep and loud. Together, we emitted a loud mix of scream and bark, "Ahhhhh!" "AarrrroooFF!!"

Mom had been at the door, watching the scene but unable to stop it. She rushed to pick me up. With pain surging from neck to shoulder, I screamed again—louder; hot tears poured onto Mom's sleeveless shoulders. I stiffened in her arms as pain accompanied each move.

"Okay, okay." She stroked my head. "Hold on, Shelly. I need you to be real still now. Okay?"

Mom left Ben with the neighbor, who'd since run to our yard after hearing the disturbance. "We may be a couple of hours, Mr. Davis," Mom told him, worry etched in her voice.

Mr. and Mrs. Davis, an older couple, had watched Ben and me on occasion since our move to Arizona. Now Mr. Davis held Ben's hand as Mom gently set me in the front seat of our car.

Mr. Davis waved us off. "Don't worry 'bout us. We'll be fine."

Dr. Douglas, our pediatrician, looked a lot like Mr. Rogers except for his starched white doctor's jacket. He always smelled good—clean, but not antiseptic. His movements were slow and deliberate. I loved Dr. Douglas and the fact that he always got down on my level, looked me in the eyes, and spoke to me as if I were an adult while he explained things with clear, simple words. He was just like Dad.

Dr. Douglas spoke to me during the X-rays, and again as he set me in an elastic brace. "We call these *wings*," he told me, referring to the brace. I wondered why I couldn't see any real wings. *Did I die? Where are the angels?* Dr. Douglas saw my apparent confusion and assured me I hadn't died but had merely broken my collarbone.

By the time we returned home, I was cranky with pain and groggy from medicine. I whined and pleaded, wanting to snuggle with my furry friend. I was sure Bambi was missing me and feeling bad about the collision.

It couldn't have been easy keeping us apart while I healed, but a few months later Bambi had puppies. Her daily runs all but disappeared, and my attention was caught up playing with her pups.

Behind the invisible veil the King looked on. The girl's features favored her grandmother's. The boy looked more like his mother, with a spray of freckles and hair that shone like copper in the sunlight.

One of the pups bit hold of the boy's pajama pants and began tugging. Unable to free himself, the boy shook with laughter. The puppy yanked again, trying to growl. The girl laughed hard, nose crinkling, falling back on her haunches, overcome with the hilarity of it all.

The King drank in the scene. Though they couldn't see or hear Him, His joyous laughter echoed their own.

Eventually more families moved into the neighborhood, and I gained a new friend. Joanna was a year younger than me, and she had a little sister, Samantha. We spent all our free time together, becoming more like siblings than friends. Our friendship would continue for the greater portion of our childhood years.

Joanna's mom, Miss Toni, became my second mom. She had no qualms telling me to eat all my vegetables whether or not my real mom made me eat them.

Miss Toni took care of cuts and scrapes and remembered whose turn it was to pick dessert. When I got stuck in the bad habit of tattling on others, Miss Toni put her foot down, telling me, "Ya know, Shell, no one wants to play with a tattletale." I may have sulked and walked home, but the next day I was knocking on Miss Toni's door to see if

Joanna could play. I learned not to be an annoying tattler and found in Miss Toni a woman who loved me as her own.

Both Mom and Miss Toni were stay-at-home moms. *That's what moms do,* I remember thinking. *They stay home to take care of their children and homes.* I didn't know anything else.

Most of our family time was spent outdoors. Our second summer in Phoenix, Dad put a pool in the backyard, doing most of the work himself. To me, it was a wonderful, giant, liquid jewel that cast moving reflections off the backside of our house. It was beautiful. We were in the pool *all* the time. The pool was a magical place for us kids. We could be anything we wanted. We were superheroes one day and dolphins the next. Suspended in the cool, silent water, we believed our abilities were endless. Ben, Joanna, and I would kick up a furious splash of water crystals that bounced on the surface. We'd dive deep to the bottom of the pool to see who could make it first while releasing giant air bubbles as human submarines. We'd then spring back to the surface, gulping air and emerging as Peter Pan and the Lost Boys or Tinker Bell, ready to explore faraway, underwater lands.

Dad would let us catch rides on his shoulders. "Hold your breath," he'd say. Then he would plunge below. I was a mermaid on the back of the great sea king; Ben was my merman brother.

If Dad wasn't too tired, we'd beg him to throw us in the air so we could hit the surface of the water with a huge splash. I can still hear Ben laughing and spewing water as he resurfaced.

Even today, the smell of chlorine takes me back to those days. I remember, too, the smell of Coppertone sunscreen. I felt so grown-up when Mom and Aunt Laurie smothered me in the sweet-smelling, greasy cocoa butter and let me lie out with them in the warm sun after hours in the cool blue water.

If we weren't in the pool, we were spending hours in the desert, exploring new trails in the foothills. The Arizona mountains offered countless adventures. Boulders and rocky cliffs were invitations for challenge and exploration. Mom would fill the picnic basket with bologna sandwiches, chips, and a jug of Kool-Aid. Then we'd pack up the station wagon, pick a mountain, and hike for hours.

Dad preferred the less-worn paths. Often, he'd make our own path along dry creeks, cactus groupings, boulders, and granite rock formations. I followed close at his heels. He stepped on a rock, and I followed. He stretched over a ravine, and I leapt. If he balanced on a fallen tree, so did I. My brother Ben, two years younger, had a harder time keeping up, but he was just as bound and determined as I was. I could see the pride in his blue eyes whenever he made it to the top of whatever boulder we were climbing only a few steps behind me.

We were on the alert for rattlers. It unnerved me that they moved so quick without legs and ate so much despite their tiny heads. Even with a chance of encountering snakes, though, we climbed the rocky paths, assured that if we stepped where Dad stepped, we'd be safe.

He watched as if He Himself were the mountain on which the little family climbed. Like a mountain, He was strong and unshakable, both a challenge and a fortress. He was the adventurer's playground, the visionary's precipice. He was, indeed, rugged, dangerous, and beautiful.

The Creator saw, heard, and felt their footsteps: the father teaching the children to ascend. The girl, watchful, learning what it meant to follow by stretching, stepping, and trusting. The boy, thrilled to be part of the excursion.

On the path, as the girl followed her father, the true Father planted a seed in her mind: "This is how you will follow Me."

As we settled into our new life in Arizona, Mom and Dad became involved with a local Lutheran church. We spent considerable time there. Dad was always working on building projects, and they both taught Sunday school classes. Church became our second home and family. This was where my first impressions of Jesus were forged.

It was during this time that Dad taught Ben and me the Lord's Prayer. While Ben was too young to care, I was really frustrated by the prayer. It had too many words for me to memorize. "I'm never gonna get it!" I whined.

Dad stood with hands on hips, studying us a moment before sitting on the floor. "Come here." He waved for me to sit on his lap. Then he went through the prayer again, verse by verse, explaining each part, as Ben scooted his plastic train in circles around us.

"*Our Father who art in heaven.* God is your real Father, Shelly. He's in heaven.

"*Hallowed be thy name.* God's not like us. He is holy. There is only good and no bad in Him.

"*Thy kingdom come.* When Jesus came to earth, He taught us about the ways of heaven.

"*Thy will be done* . . . God wants us to live those ways.

"*. . . on earth as it is in heaven.* Heaven is a real place.

"*Give us this day* . . . God is the One who makes sure we have the things we need to live.

"*. . . our daily bread* . . . He gives us what we need, when we truly need it.

"*. . . and forgive us our trespasses* . . . We sin, Shelly. Sin is when we do things that are wrong or hurtful, to ourselves, others, and even God. We need to let Him know we're sorry when we do.

"*. . . as we forgive those who trespass against us.* Jesus teaches us to forgive people who do wrong to us.

"*And lead us not into temptation* . . . God wants us to ask for His help when we are tempted to do the wrong thing.

"*. . . but deliver us from evil.* God will protect us from bad things as we look to Him.

"*For thine is the kingdom* . . . God made everything, Shelly. It all belongs to Him.

"*. . . and the power* . . . It's important we remember that God's power is different than man's power.

" *. . . and the glory* . . . Glory. That's something you'll have to learn. Glory is proof of God's goodness. It's everywhere, but not everybody sees it.

" *. . . for ever and ever.* God and His goodness never end."

Ben was oblivious, off in his own thoughts and imagination. "Choo choo!" he said, sweeping between Dad and me.

I continued to think about what Dad had said. Instead of trying to memorize the words, I thought about what each part meant. Mom or Dad continued to lead me through the prayer each night, discussing the different parts, and eventually I was able to memorize it after all.

♕

From across the surface of the planet, prayers shimmered before Him like stars lighting the darkness, and in their shimmering He heard a melody too beautiful for man's ears to perceive.

He watched and listened in delight to the thoughts and words of strong and weak alike, cherishing the sincerity of the young and innocent as well as the earnestness of the old and feeble.

"Beautiful, My children—beautiful! Talk to me; pray to Me; sing to Me. I want to hear from you!"

And in the hearts of the two children struggling to learn and understand His Son's prayer, He whispered a promise: "These words, like little seeds, will grow in your hearts, and as they do, you will come into a greater understanding of Me."

Our little church had a small youth group but no youth leader. As

Mom and Dad began spending time getting to know the kids at our church, they grew to care deeply about the cares and concerns of the young people in our church and community. Before long they officially became leaders for the group.

I loved it when the "big kids" came to the house. There was excitement in the air whenever they were with us. I could tell we were part of something bigger than ourselves, though I didn't understand what it was. I watched as my parents cared for the young people and took their challenges to heart. I could see they really cared for these kids. This made me proud. I loved listening to them talk excitedly over plans they'd made for road trips, campouts, teachings, and outreaches. I knew Mom and Dad loved us, but I saw that they also loved these kids, and the kids loved them. For Ben and me, being a younger part of the youth group was one new adventure after another. The group went camping and to Disneyland and the Gulf of Mexico with Ben and me in tow. It was a family thing.

Besides their ministry dream of leading youth into a vibrant relationship with Christ, Mom and Dad had another dream as well. They wanted to adopt a child. As a young boy, Dad had been invited to his Sunday school teacher's home for her little boy's birthday. She and her husband had adopted the boy from China. It made an impression on Dad that carried into fatherhood.

Mom and Dad could have more children naturally, but they earnestly wanted to give a home and family to a child who didn't have one. At the time I didn't know what a missionary was, but Dad said, "You can be a missionary without going anywhere. If there is room in your heart and room in your home, you can live on mission your whole life."

One night, after baths and story time, Mom and Dad sat Ben and me down. They had something special to tell us.

"Guess what?" Dad said.

My hair was still wet from my bath. "Mom, can I have a ponytail?"

Mom sprayed Johnson's No More Tears on my locks and began combing my hair.

Dad said, "We're going to get a new baby."

"What?!" I screamed excitedly. Ben was too young to understand, but I was elated. "A baby?!"

Mom pulled my hair into the twisty tie. It always felt like my face was being stretched in order to get my hair in place. She turned my shoulders to see my face. "Yes, Shelly. Whattaya think about that?"

A new baby! I could hardly believe it. "Is the baby already in your tummy?" I looked at Mom's small waist. She didn't look pregnant. Dad explained that we were going to adopt a baby from a faraway country.

I thought all moms got to stay home to raise their children. It never occurred to me that a mother would have to give away her child in order to provide a home and a life that she could not provide herself. This was a challenging new idea.

As I absorbed the reality, I grieved for both the mom and the child. I hope my Mom and Dad knew what a precious and powerful revelation this was to their children. It is a gift for a child to understand that she has what others may not be so fortunate to have. As I continued processing the news and all that it meant, it dawned on me that I got to share my family with this baby!

I asked Mom how soon the baby would come. She explained, "It may take a while. We'll just have to see." That night we prayed together as a family for "our baby."

In Sunday school, Ben and I sang the words to a familiar chorus:

Red, brown, yellow, black and white;
they are precious in His sight.
Jesus loves the little children of the world.

Now the song was personal. I could barely wait to meet my new sister.

Mom and Dad contacted the Holt International Adoption Agency. Holt served as a liaison between a Korean foster home, the Korean government, the US government, and Mom and Dad. They led us through the process, and eventually we became a match for a baby girl from South Korea. I was going to have a baby sister.

Once the match was made, we were given limited information. We received an envelope with basic details on her approximate birthday, health, and orphanage. Inside the information packet were two photos of our new baby. The photos were barely two inches square.

For me, they were a promise of my soon-to-be sister. Mom graciously let me handle the pictures each time we showed the photos and shared the news with people we knew. We showed Miss Toni and Joanna, church friends, neighbors, my teacher and classmates, the baker, and anyone else who would listen.

It seemed to take forever to get through the interviews and processing. We waited with anticipation. Mom bought a pretty, lace-edged baby dress for our baby's journey home. Mom and Dad included Ben and me in decorating her room.

At Christmas, Mom asked me for help. "I need a special gift, and I'm wondering if you could help me find one? The church is collecting gifts for children who don't have very much. Dad and I thought you might like to help."

Through the adoption process, Ben and I were becoming more aware that there were children in other places who lived differently than us and often with less. Now Mom wanted my help in caring for them. "Yeah!" I said. "That sounds like fun."

Mom paused at the stove and looked at me, "This has to be a special gift because we can only send one gift for each child. It has to be really good."

I wondered which store would have something *really special*.

"Where should we go?" I asked, thinking maybe we would need to go to the big Christown shopping mall.

Mom turned to study me. Her eyes met mine. "Well, I'm thinking you could help me find something that's really special to you, something that belongs to you that you would be willing to give to someone who doesn't have toys."

One of my own toys? I didn't expect that.

Mom responded to the glazed look in my eyes. "It's not easy to give away something that is special to us, but it makes the gift"—Mom paused, smiled to herself, and tried a new word on me—"exceptional."

Dad walked in and picked up on the conversation. "That's how God gives. Remember: He gave us Jesus, His only Son. He wants us to be like Him. He's less concerned with things that don't really matter to us. It's the things that mean the most to us that matter, because then it comes from the heart." He looked at me to see if I was absorbing what he was saying.

Mom handed me forks to set the table. "Why don't you think about it and see what comes to mind."

They wanted me to take the time to count the cost. "Think about it carefully and pray before you choose," Dad added. "When you find that special gift, Mom will show you how to wrap it yourself. You can place it under the tree at church. It will your gift."

Dad had just read a story to Ben and me about the wise men bringing gifts to Jesus. "They gave the best they had," he had said. "God gave His best, too—He gave us Jesus."

I considered my favorite toys. I could give any of them away happily—except for one. I knew what my best was.

I had a baby doll that looked and felt *real*—Baby Tender Love. My friends thought she was the best. I remember one of my friend's moms actually offered to trade dolls or toys in exchange for her. Her daughter *really* liked my Baby Tender Love, and they weren't in stores any longer.

The truth was I didn't really play with toys or dolls. I mostly played outdoors and used my imagination, but I knew Baby Tender Love was special. I had a queasy feeling in my stomach. How could I give her up? She was the best I had. Suddenly, she seemed to matter even more.

I decided to give my *second* best. Surely my second best would be appreciated by someone who didn't have *anything*. The next day I convinced myself, Mom, and Dad that I had found the perfect gift.

"Lucy" was a tall, stiff, hard plastic doll with pretty blue eyes and ugly hair. She looked brand-new because no one wanted to play with her!

"She's not as soft as Baby Tender Love, but she's newer, and look! She blinks." I proudly showed Mom, glossing over my selfish decision to keep Baby Tender Love to myself. I added convincingly, "I think she'll make a special gift."

Mom helped me wrap Lucy. Mine was one of the biggest packages under the tree. I was proud to present such a large gift. Mom was pleased, but I knew the truth. Deep inside, I felt something that didn't feel good. I'd withheld my best.

That secret decision haunted me for years. I still look back now and recognize my old selfish nature that continues to pop up, wanting to keep the best for myself.

The Great Gift Giver watched the parents planting seeds in the hearts of their children. He smiled at their wisdom.

"Yes, yes!

"Ah but look: she chose a lesser gift." He walked beside the girl as she awkwardly carried the large package to lay it among others. He saw her inner disappointment.

"No, My love, that was not your best; that's why your heart hurts. Giving

to others is one of the greatest gifts you will ever receive. But true sacrificial giving comes with growth, and as you grow you will have more opportunities to experience that blessing. For now, My grace is sufficient."

He looked around at the other gifts: priceless gifts, cheap gifts, secondhand gifts, and sacrificial gifts.

He was still beside the girl as she laid her gift beneath the tree and walked back to her family. "You will have more to give, My dear," He said with great love in His voice. "I will teach you to give your best."

As time drew closer for our baby's adoption to be complete, I thought about my new sister. How was her momma able to give her up? I figured that momma must have an enormous heart to give *her* very best: a real baby. Would I ever have such a heart?

Finally, it was time for our family to receive our special gift. It was more than talk and prayers. Our baby was ready to come home.

Grandma G and Uncle Don flew in from Missouri. They came to watch Ben and me while Mom and Dad flew to get our baby sister. *A new sister!*

Her name was Ahn Bok Dong, but we were giving her a new name that would be easier for her in America—Jennifer Ahn.

I had told anyone and everyone who would listen to me that we were getting a new baby sister. This wasn't just any new baby. She was special because God was bringing her from the other side of the world to be with us.

The following week, Mom and Dad returned home with Jenny. I couldn't wait to hold her.

Mom had me sit on our black vinyl couch with a blanket. She placed Jenny in my arms and handed me a bottle, showing me how to handle the little bundle.

I fell in love. We had prayed for her so many times, and now here she was, in my arms. The thought crossed my mind, *Would I ever know how to give such gifts?*

They said she was small for her age, but she was heavy in my arms, squirming all around. She seemed really big to me, and I couldn't wait for her to grow more. Jenny was five months old when she arrived, with a messy crop of spiky, black hair. Physically and cognitively, she was more like a three-month-old. She couldn't roll over or sit on her own. She'd had limited mobility and attention at the orphanage.

She continued to wriggle in my arms, but eventually she settled down and took the bottle. Jenny gazed back at me with charcoal eyes. She was beautiful. This was my *sister.*

I studied her face, amazed that she was just now meeting her family. That day I whispered to her, committing to always do my part to take care of her no matter what happened. She would never be without a home again.

Jenny quickly made up for her developmental lack. She grew strong physically and sharp cognitively. She caught up to children her age and then surpassed them. Jenny thrived with love and care.

Soon we were back to potlucks and campouts with Mom and Dad's pastoral adventures. Now we had one more in the bunch.

The face of the Father shined as He looked down on the growing family. Family. Adoption! "Children, I have adopted you. You are Mine."

He looked at His Son, laughing with a child in His arms. He noted the beautiful scars on His wrists, before looking back to the children of earth. "My Son traveled far and paid much for you to be adopted into My family."

He was pleased to see His reflection in them. His glory resonated through their laughter and compassion.

As they walked in His ways, His Spirit forged an unseen wall of peace and favor, protecting them, but He also saw into the future and knew what they didn't.

Everything they were and had would soon be challenged.

Fall sunsets in Arizona are amazing. They are rich in purple, pink, crimson, orange, and amber. Fall also marks the beginning of dove hunting. When the desert skies were wrapping up the days in brilliant color, Dad would get out his gun and prime it for hunting. The oily scent of gun cleaner on old diaper rags lingered in the air.

Dad watched me studying his regimen. "You know what, kiddo? If you'd get to where you could do your homework without all the fuss, I might just take you with me."

Homework was a challenge for me. Constantly. It wasn't that I wasn't willing to do it, it was that I had such a hard time understanding it. But Dad was making an offer I couldn't refuse. I knew there was no room for whiners in Dad's truck—especially not on a hunt. He buffed the metal and glanced at me again.

"It can be dangerous," he cautioned, "and you have to be very quiet. You have to do exactly as I tell you." He looked at me, his eyebrows raised as if in a question. "We'll be out there for a long time, ya know."

I was too excited to say anything. I simply nodded. I believe I was in second grade. From then on, in the true spirit of a "nerd-venturer," I crept from room to room, practicing my hunt crouch.

Of course, I was too young to handle a gun. Dad rarely even let me hold the ammunition; but once I proved good on my efforts at homework, he agreed to bring me as his helper.

The day of a hunt finally came. Dad handed me leather gloves. "You need these to pick 'em up, and this to carry 'em in." He handed me a leather-strapped satchel we'd purchased in Mexico during a campout with the church group. The straps hung low on me, so I slung it crossways over my shoulder. I rubbed the braided strap with my fingers. I was a warrior princess.

We stood in a broad field, watching the sky and listening in the quiet. Occasionally we'd hear the fire of another hunter. Following the aim of Dad's rifle and the proximity of the fallen bird, I waited for his lead. "Okay, Shell," he finally said. "Go get it."

The first time I found one still alive, I panicked. I ran back to Dad, afraid to pick up the injured bird. He followed me back to where the bird lay. Dad slowly stooped down on one knee, picked up the half-living, half-dying bird, and said, "Sorry, little guy."

In his quiet voice, he explained that we needed to let it die quickly so it wouldn't suffer. "You're not gonna like this, but it's what we got to do."

He held the body with one hand, and with the other he quickly torqued its neck, mercifully ending its struggle. My stomach turned.

"Dad, you don't want me to do that, do you? I mean, I don't think I can."

He stayed scrunched down at my level and lifted the flap on the satchel, gently placing the dove beside the others. Then he returned his gaze to mine.

"Well," he said, "it probably will happen again. It's not an easy thing, but it's the kind thing. The sooner we help it go, the kinder it is to the creature. We couldn't just leave it there in pain, now, could we?"

Dad's crystal blue eyes met mine. He hadn't answered my question. I knew he would do it if I couldn't, but he was also giving me the chance to do something really hard. Of course, I didn't *want* to, but the thought of letting a dove suffer weighed heavy on me. Gently, Dad was stretching my world again.

That was all I could think about the next time we went out. Once our truck pulled into the fields west of Sixty-Seventh Avenue, I blurted out, "Dad, if it happens again, you know, if one of 'em doesn't die right away, I think I need to do it."

I paused, putting my hair into a ponytail. "But I'm gonna need your help."

He squeezed my shoulder and said, "Yeah. Sure thing." Silently, I prayed we wouldn't have the opportunity.

We'd been out for a while, and the morning haze was almost gone. I took my jacket off and tied it around my waist. Dad had several good hits. "Couple more shots, then we go," he said.

My ponytail had come undone again, but it didn't matter; we were almost done. I was relieved as I scurried toward an old wire fence where the last dove had fallen.

Then my heart sank. The dove circled helplessly on the dirt, attempting to flutter away. I turned back to Dad.

"Dad!" I looked again at the dying bird, "Help."

Dad made his way over. I tried to pick up the bird, but it fluttered too much for my timid hands.

"Dad . . ." I whispered, terrified. "What if I do it wrong?"

He stooped down and gently picked it up. "You want to do this?"

I didn't, but I nodded yes. I crouched beside him. Dad was peaceful, so I was too.

"Okay. We hold its body firm like this." He spoke patiently, guiding my hand with his one free hand. I could tell he, too, wanted this to be done. We both could sense fear in the little creature in my hands.

They didn't recognize His presence as He stood in the field with them, though He was the soft breeze blowing the girl's hair about her face as she and her father held life and death in their hands.

Watching the man and child, He considered the day His Son bore the weight of death as He faced His final breath so many seasons ago.

The Father leaned down where the dove had fallen and picked up a few grains of wheat; the field was ripe and ready to be reaped. The adjacent field had just been harvested.

That year, Mom and Dad pulled me from public school and placed me in Martin Luther Parochial School.

It was midyear of second grade. No one explained *why*, but I'm sure they were trying to help me be more successful in school. I believe Dad recognized that I needed extra scholastic help.

Dad worked with me as I labored through anything to do with school. I struggled both in the classroom and at home with homework. I didn't understand things. I seemed to process concepts differently than the other kids.

Mom was encouraging and optimistic, but Dad seemed to understand my battle. Yet despite Dad's gentle and patient nature, I think I pushed even him to exasperation.

The teacher-to-student ratio was better at the new school, but I still struggled. I agonized each time a new concept was taught. When I finally grasped addition, the other students were finishing subtraction. Once I grasped subtraction, they were mastering multiplication tables. The same applied with reading, science, and cursive.

Trying to understand sentence structure made my head spin. I liked to read for fun, but if it was part of learning and if there was a timeline, I was doomed. I was *very* slow.

This continued throughout my school years. Learning new concepts was perplexing. I couldn't grasp things. I wanted to understand and do well, but things simply didn't click.

It was more than frustrating; I began to believe there was something wrong with me.

One memory from second grade sticks out from the others.

The school was quite small. In the afternoons, first and second grades were combined in one classroom with one teacher. Once I figured out that the first-grade classroom was vacant when lunch and recess began, I had the brilliant idea to get a friend and make our own indoor playground while everyone else was outside.

While the kids and the teachers were out on the playground, my friend and I pushed all the desks around to make tunnels. On our hands and knees, wiggling through the desk legs, we crawled through the forest of "trees," eluding the "giants" who chased us. We entered secret caverns in search of hidden treasures. Desks became mountains we dared to climb over. Giggling through our adventure, we ran and chased and clambered about. We played and laughed our heads off.

I was so proud to have found the perfect secret playground.

But we never put the desks and chairs back afterwards, and it was only a few days before Mrs. Kruger, the pastor's wife and our teacher, figured out who had made the secret playground.

I was so scared I almost peed my pants wondering how many swats we would get for our shenanigans. Nothing ever came of it except that the first-grade door was always locked from then on, and Mrs. Kruger personally escorted us to the playground.

I'm pretty sure I never looked at her face directly again after that.

He sat on the teacher's desk, grinning with pleasure, as the girls laughed and chased each other 'round and 'round the desk.

The girls were clueless to His quiet presence, too absorbed in their innocent laughter.

"Run, girls, run. Yes. Exercise your minds and creativity. Explore! I think, My darlin's, that I will tuck this memory into your hearts. One day you will reach deep down in darkness and find this rare and hidden jewel. I want you to look upon this time of innocence and see who I created you to be."

His eyes softened.

"A time is coming when you will leave these carefree ways, but one day I will bring you back."

In third grade I could participate in Band. Mom signed me up and rented a clarinet. She was excited, and so was I. Finally! Here was a subject that wouldn't strain my brain.

Or so I thought. Our excitement faded quickly. It was the whole "new concept" issue all over again.

Notes? Scales? Different shapes made different sounds? Everything was literal for me. It didn't make sense that a circle with a hole in it would sound different from a filled circle at the end of a stick. Some notes even had "feathers" on them, and that was supposed to *mean something*?

These were words and symbols, not *sounds*. None of it made sense. I couldn't make the connection and I felt stupid. The funny part was, the band teacher didn't check to see if I was getting it. I just blew and blew. No good sound came from my horn. I participated in two or three band presentations before I could no longer stand moving my fingers around, pretending I knew where they were supposed to go. I knew I wasn't playing. Why didn't anyone else? I felt like an idiot, and I hated faking it. I didn't sign up the next semester.

School challenges weighed me down, but something more was pressing down on life as I knew it. I was mostly unaware except for the nagging feeling something was *off*. Mom and Dad seemed preoccupied. We didn't go to church as much.

Maybe it was just that Mom had a new job. Things were just a little different somehow.

The Great Musician saw the girl and the horn she had cast down on the floor

in frustration. He saw two vessels. Picking up the girl in His mighty hands, He peered past her tear-smeared face and deep into her eyes.

He saw her imperfections and weaknesses. "What you see as challenges will one day serve to amplify the song I place within you," He said tenderly. "Mastering obstacles is necessary practice to perfect the beauty of My melody in you.

"You are My instrument. One day you'll see. I have made you the way you are—with purpose. You were made to worship Me. Your life will be a song unto Me."

The little girl knelt beside her bed and prayed before drifting off to sleep. The Creator captured her words and wove them into His own song.

Unseen to the eyes of those below, unheard to their dull ears, the Master spun on course with the sun and moon. The stars echoed His songs through the night as He sang a beautiful song of love and promise over His children.

2

THE BROKEN ROAD

$\mathcal{I}$ was eight years old, and it was 1975—the same glorious year that Bubble Yum came out. Ben was six and Jenny was four. I saved my allowance to buy pack after pack of that fabulous gum. I'd buy four or five packs at a time in case the stores ran out. It was so soft, squishy, and packed with sweetness. Bubble Yum was the latest craze, and it was *amazing*. Jenny thought so too.

Jenny *loved* chewing gum—any kind. Bubble Yum, Trident, Bazooka, gumballs . . . it didn't matter the type. She just loved gum. She would even pick it up off the street or out from under a table and stick it in her mouth. Ben and I would roll our eyes when we caught her. "Gross, Jenny!" we would say, sometimes nearly in unison. She didn't care. Gum was her thing.

Jenny knew Bubble Yum was the best for bubbles. She also liked to squish it between her fingers. More than once, it got tangled in her long, silky, black hair. Mom had the hardest time getting it out.

One afternoon Mom had an especially difficult time getting a huge, sticky wad out of my sister's hair. In a huff, she went to the drawer, pulled out scissors, and cut the wad from Jen's pigtail. She snipped the other pig tail to even it out. Later, when Jen took her hair down, it was all uneven and Mom had to cut a bunch more off to get it back to a decent shape.

I liked sharing Bubble Yum with Ben, Jen, and kids at school. "But keep it in your mouth," I'd warn. Ben and Jenny were really the best friends I had. We'd moved from our old neighborhood, so I didn't see Joanna except on special occasions.

Going to a private school made it hard to make friends in the neighborhood, and my classmates lived in different parts of the city.

There was one girl in my class I really admired. Everyone liked Kristen. She was fun, pretty, smart, and kind. I wanted to be like her. I tried to dress like her and watched everything she did so I could be more like her. Then something happened to Kristen.

The once-lively, outgoing girl changed. Her smile was gone, and she appeared empty. Kristen seemed to be "missing," even though she was still five desks in front of me.

That fall her mom invited me to Kristen's surprise birthday party. That's when I found out her parents were getting a divorce.

After the party I avoided Kristen. I was afraid of her. How could she change so much? It was as though she was contagious with a disease I wanted nothing to do with. That wouldn't happen to me or *my* family. Family stayed together.

The truth was, things felt different at my house. Mom and Dad were acting strange. They didn't talk like they used to. When Dad came home after work, the mood was quiet and serious. The laughter was gone; a cold quietness took its place. Somehow, I felt responsible.

Gone was the lightheartedness that once filled our home. Family friends didn't come over like they used to. Mom and Dad were no longer leading the youth group. Somewhere along the way, we'd stopped going to church entirely.

I would catch Mom crying, trying to hide her tears. I squirmed inside as I watched my parents weaken and turn to friends for comfort instead of each other.

Later that year, Mom told me she and Dad were getting a divorce. I willed the words away, not wanting to believe it; but like gum in Jenny's hair, it was there, and you couldn't ignore it. You only got messy trying to fix it.

I wondered how our lives would get cut and snipped out of shape.

The Kinsman-Redeemer saw the entanglement when it began. He had sent warning messages to the couple's hearts, but his warnings had gone unheard and unanswered. He knew a cutting apart would follow. It would crush and wound everyone involved, and He would share the pain of each precious adult and child.

Mom had asked Dad for a divorce. She told him she'd simply fallen out of love. I remember her telling me, "Sometimes people just fall out of love and there's nothing you can do about it."

I didn't buy it. They'd taught me too much about love and how it is a gift you give someone else. You weren't supposed to take gifts back.

One night after Dad moved out, I heard whispers in the living room. Why had Dad come to visit *after* we'd gone to bed? I got up to go say hi. Of course, he'd want to see me.

As I walked down the hall, the orange shag carpet crushed beneath my toes, hiding the sound of my footsteps. *Why was he here so late?* Maybe he and Mom were going to finally going to talk this thing out.

Hope rose in me, and it dawned on me that they might need to talk privately. If we kids were awake, we would be a distraction from this important conversation. I'd honor their special time alone, but I needed confirmation. I'd been praying for this.

The lights were dim, and they were talking in whispers.

What are they saying? They sound happy. Mom's laughing.

I felt a smile grow on my face. It was silly because I wasn't smiling at anyone, but it felt good to feel hope and happiness for a change. I wanted to dash out and join the happy moment, but I kept back. *Don't break the spell.*

I strained to hear. There was a pause in the whispers, so I peeked my head around the corner to see. He was at the door. Was he leaving already? I almost blurted out, "Dad, wait!" but I refrained and watched.

They were in each other's arms. They kissed. But something didn't make sense. I felt the smile fade from my face.

Something was wrong? What was it?

I looked harder and saw. My stomach lurched, and my knees buckled. My legs felt like noodles. I held on to the wall for support.

That's not Dad.

Noooo!

I willed my legs to work and ran back to my room, careful not to make any noise. Back in the safety of my bed, I clutched at the sheets—angry, hurt, and confused.

I was appalled. I couldn't sleep, trying to process the image of the kiss and the sound of muffled laughter playing over and over in my head.

The truth was (and she would later tell Dad), Mom had messed up. Afterward, her guilty conscience weighed too heavy, and she couldn't see herself as worthy of redemption for having broken her marriage vows. Maybe Dad would have forgiven her, but she didn't tell him till it was too late. She never gave him the chance.

Sometimes we think we can protect our kids from the truth. And sometimes they find out.

I lost more than the feeling in my legs that night. I lost hope. A bit of innocence was lost that night too. I thought about Dad, Ben, and Jenny. What if any of them had seen what I saw? I couldn't bear the thought of them having to carry that picture in their minds.

I told no one. Instead, I silently committed to guard Ben, Jenny —and Dad.

I became more serious, endeavoring to take on the role of protector and nurturer to Ben and Jenny. Mom and Dad were too busy trying to pick up pieces of their own broken selves.

The Holy One grieved as the child stumbled back to her bed in the night.

Hearts lay strewn at His feet.

The woman, tormented by the sins of her past, had turned from Him. In reckless brokenness she'd trampled on her own heart.

The husband's heart, too, was crushed, bruised, and broken.

The child's heart lay feverishly pulsing on the floor in the darkened hall.

The Holy One's anger rose and burned. Not at any of His beloved children, but at the deceiver who had lured them to this place. His eyes blazed seeing the broken dreams and lost hope. He let out a roar that echoed throughout the unseen kingdom.

"Marriage. Covenant. Family. These are MINE!"

With a heavy heart, the Great King quietly leaned down, picking up the battered hearts. He counted the cost that lay ahead for them.

In a whisper, He breathed grace onto all, then tenderly tucked each heart back into place.

He collected the child's tears and spoke over her in the black of the night, "You are MINE, and one day you will know you are Mine. You will walk upright in dark places.

"I will teach you to forgive, to trust, and to hope again."

I never saw the man again. Years later I learned that Mom never saw him again either once the divorce was final.

Mom and Dad's divorce finalized in the early spring of 1975. Mom felt too guilt ridden to turn back.

My mom was a pretty woman with short, blonde, sassy hair and a shapely physique. She had smiling eyes that sometimes appeared light blue and other times looked green. Her nature was kind and unassuming. When men found out that she was single, they would ask her out.

I hated that. Dad was the only man I wanted in Mom's life. It was tough letting go despite broken hope.

Why couldn't we just move on without some new intruder adding to our disjointed brokenness?

Mom started dating a man named Nick. The second time I met him, he told me he wanted to show me something very special, but I'd have to wait till the next time he came to the house. I wasn't sure about that.

"What is it?" I asked with hesitation. It sounded sketchy. Why should I trust him? Was he going to be kissing on Mom too?

He just smiled and said, "It's a good thing. You'll like it."

After school a few days later, I asked, "Mom, when's Mr. Potato coming back?"

She looked at me and laughed. "It's Mr. Portillo. Por-TILL-o. He's coming over tomorrow night. Do you like him?"

I shrugged. "I don't know."

The truth was, he'd piqued my curiosity with the whole "show you something special" deal. Despite my mistrust, I was hungry for something special.

Nick came the next evening. It was strange—a man openly coming to spend time with Mom. She belonged with Dad. This was his house, too. The chair at the end of the table was Dad's. I just wanted Dad to come home and have dinner and resume life as we'd known it. My thoughts always trailed back to Dad.

Nick was asking me a question. "Do you remember that I told you I wanted to show you something very special?" I knew he was trying to win my approval. What could he possibly know about special? My dad was special. Dad was all I wanted.

"Shelly, I want you to see one of the most beautiful girls you could ever meet."

That wasn't what I was expecting.

How could he know such a beautiful girl? I wondered. *Where is she, and how does he know her? Does he know a supermodel? No . . . This has got to be some kind of trick.*

"Hold on. I have something in my car for you. I'll be right back."

I half-expected him to have a friend in the car—someone who was famous—though that didn't seem likely. He didn't seem like someone who would know anyone famous. And why would a famous person care about meeting an eight-year-old girl?

Maybe he has a picture of someone famous.

I knew there was a hook somewhere, but I wasn't keen enough to process this new line of thinking.

He returned with a brown paper bag and handed it to me. "Go ahead. Open it."

Oh. Yup. It's gonna be a magazine. He's weird. I don't understand. What's the point here?

Puzzled, I reached into the bag, and instead of a magazine, I grabbed a handle. I pulled the object out. It was a mirror. I tilted my head in question, feeling more than slightly awkward. It's strange to look at yourself in a mirror, especially in front of someone you barely know.

"There she is. Do you see her?" He asked, smiling with raised eyebrows, looking expectantly at me.

I didn't see a beautiful girl. I just saw *me*—a sad, freckle-nosed, blue-eyed girl. I didn't know what to say. I felt awkward in a way I had not experienced before. Still, Nick had taken extra care to reach out to me. That *kind of* made me feel special.

That month Mom moved us from our house to a townhome on the

other end of town, close to my school. Dad had already moved into an apartment of his own. This last change was yet another door closing on the life of our family. It was strange to move to a place to which Dad had no attachment. With each passing day, I felt further and further from Dad.

The Unchanging One stood near, watching and observing the changes.

To the woman He whispered, "Daughter, you can stop this now. You are off track. It's not too late. Don't buy the lies you hear. Repent. Do not embrace the shame that you feel. I long to free you from that."

To the man He said firmly, "Now is the time to press in. They need you. Don't pull back."

Mom and Nick became more serious. They worked in the same office, so their professional and social lives intersected. Nick was soon part of our everyday lives.

One day in late spring, they went on a quick overnight trip to Las Vegas for a special promotional event. When they returned the next day, I came downstairs and noticed a shiny new addition on the bookshelf in the family room.

What's that?

There, next to Mom's hardbound books, was a clock made of dice. It was obviously some sort of prize from Las Vegas—and totally out of place with our décor. Immediately, I disliked the flashy clock. There were enough new things to get used to. This clock was just one more thing that didn't fit right.

Mom came in the room and saw me eyeing the new clock. There was something different in her expression, something I couldn't read. I put on a cheerful voice and said, "How was your trip?"

"It was good," she said as she picked up a towel from a pile of clean laundry on the couch and began to fold it. There was something she wasn't saying. We both knew our lives were changing. It seemed Mom was caught between what had been and where we were going.

How do us kids fit in this?

She saw my unspoken question as I looked at the clock, then back at her. It was more than a clock. The red dice on slick, black plexiglass was for me a marker of a change of season. Mom loved us kids. I saw it in her eyes. She simply didn't know what to do with the circumstances.

I didn't either. I only knew we were moving forward into a season of unknown.

The Ancient of Days saw the clock and considered the scene. He could see the days and years that lay ahead.

The Great King could have stepped in. But that was not His way. He would neither coddle nor force His ways.

For Him, time was a vehicle through which truth, life, and goodness could eventually be unveiled. He allowed every person the power of choice. Would they stay on course, allowing time to reveal the good things He had in store for them? Or would they become impatient, seeking shortcuts, and reaping pain in the process?

Nick was Italian, with a sharp tongue and quick wit. He looked nothing like my father. Dad was lean, with a long torso, straight black hair, and blue eyes set deep in a freckled face. You couldn't really tell Dad's face was freckled because it was ruggedly ruddy. I was fond of that face and his gentle mannerisms. He walked with his toes slightly pointed outward, his feet and legs a little extended before his hips.

Occasionally, he would sweep his hands in a slow expressive way as he talked.

Nick, on the other hand, had a thick torso with a little belly, though he was very strong. His hands were short and thick, especially his thumbs. He was not as tall as Dad and had black, wiry hair that was beginning to gray at the temples, revealing the nine-year difference between his age and Mom's. There were traces in his strong Italian features that hinted he may have been handsome in his youth. All I saw was an old man. His voice was loud with a crackly tone.

Nick liked to cook Italian dishes and was really good at it. We warmed up to him as he entertained us with stories and homemade pizzas and calzones. Before long, Nick was at the house all the time.

On Mother's Day, Mom invited Nick's parents over for dinner. Marie and Tony were first-generation immigrants. They were proud to tell how they had come to America on a ship from Italy. Marie, a master cook, brought dinner. It was a feast of one amazing dish after another. We had antipasto, stuffed mushrooms, veal parmigiana, lasagna, and *crocchette di patate*. For dessert she served homemade sponge cake. It was the first time I had real whipped cream frosting. I'd never eaten so much at one time. Every time I looked at Miss Marie, she raised her eyebrows, extending a smile and a dish of food. "You want more?"

Mom looked at me after they left. "So, what'd ya think?"

I shrugged. "Well, they're really nice, and I think Miss Marie should open a restaurant. I guess they're okay."

I could see Mom cared what I thought, and it was important to her that I liked them. It was obvious she wanted this to be a positive experience.

In truth, Nick's parents were a welcome buffer to all the changes. With all the disjointedness of broken and new relationships, Miss Marie offered something different. She was short, round, and motherly, as well as warm and caring. She opened her arms wide, embracing us kids with big hugs as if we were family from the very beginning. We were her little chickadees. Tony sang goofy songs and made us feel at ease in our own new environment.

After that, Miss Marie often invited us over for special meals. As we sat around the table, finishing the last course, she told stories about her Italy. I imagined the faraway land and people, adding it to my list of "one day" places to explore. My real grandparents were in St. Louis, so having someone to dote on us was a welcome treat.

As the hot summer days rolled on, Mom and Nick became nearly inseparable. We had a huge community pool, so we spent most of the summer hanging out poolside. I missed Dad's presence and the games we had played together in the water.

Now it was Nick who was with us in the pool. Nick taught us Marco Polo and gave us tips so we could stay underwater longer. He taught us special dives, and he offered rides on his shoulders underwater, but somehow it just didn't feel right.

He earnestly liked to have fun and worked at making sure everyone present was having a good time. Part of me wanted to like him, but part of me didn't. Dad was still my hero.

Once school started, Nick took Mom on a road trip to San Diego to relax and recover a bit from the upheaval of the last year. He was pursuing her.

From my naïve perspective, I thought that Mom being courted was like a vacation for her. Mom seemed to adjust more easily to this new life, whereas I scrambled, picking up fragmented pieces of my own identity.

I never thought Mom was actually in love with Nick. In truth, I believe she was doing her best to assure that a semblance of normalcy continued in our lives by finding someone to help shoulder financial responsibility.

Even so, it felt as though Ben, Jenny, and I were stuck in the backseat of a cosmic time machine, watching strange events and scenes we didn't understand. We were on a new journey without a clue where we were going.

The King knew where they were going. They ignored every warning sign around them.

"Slow down!"

"Caution."

"YIELD!"

"Road Work Ahead."

They pressed on, focusing on their own plans.

The Wise One would not interfere. He watched and waited.

Nick came by one afternoon after their trip. He had a flat paper bag from Kodak. "Hey, come see what I have." He called Ben, Jenny, and I to the kitchen as he pulled out photos of Mom. She was all dressed up in a garden I'd never seen before. It was obvious this was from their trip to San Diego.

Nick wanted to show her off. "Isn't she beautiful?" he beamed.

Mom was all dressed up in fancy clothes. The photos were really pretty, but I was confused.

Why don't I like these? That's my Mom. I love her. She looks so pretty. Shouldn't I be happy? I forced myself to say something. "Yeah, wow, Mom. These are really nice."

I didn't recognize the feeling, but I was jealous. I was jealous that Nick was the one Mom was smiling for in the photos. This was a whole new category of thoughts and emotions I wasn't prepared to deal with. The pictures left me feeling lonely and, suddenly, further away from Mom.

I missed the days of Mom always being home—there for us kids.

Now Nick was the one who captivated Mom's attention. He was pursuing her, and that made me uncomfortable. I couldn't stop or prevent it. Where would it lead?

Nick seemed to pick up on my wariness as I studied the photos. He tilted his head to me and said, "You are beautiful, just like your Mom." His way of comforting only left me feeling hollow.

One afternoon a few weeks later, I went downstairs to get a snack. Mom was in the kitchen, all dressed up. I figured she had just come from an appointment with a client. "Hi, Mom."

She turned toward me with an awkward smile. "Hi. Whatcha been up to this afternoon?"

I grabbed a snack cake from the pantry. "Homework." That was half-true. I had opened up my math book, but my thoughts side-tracked, and I hadn't actually gotten any of it done.

"Oh, that reminds me." She reached in her purse and pulled out a packet of pencil erasers. "Here you go." I constantly wore down the erasers on pencils, always second-guessing my answers. Homework was more of a struggle than ever. It was a challenge to stay focused because my thoughts always trailed back into the abyss of trying to figure out the changes going on around me. My papers were messy, with gray pencil marks and tattered tears where I had written, erased, and rewritten over and over. It was embarrassing to turn in work. I took the erasers. "Thanks."

Mom attempted another smile. Something was off. What was up with this awkwardness? "Go get Ben and Jenny. Nick will be here in a few minutes, and we want to share some news with you." She turned too quickly, and her eyes didn't meet mine.

My legs got that funny jelly feeling again.

News?

"Okay, sure," I said and my mouth felt dry. The prospect of more news left me feeling like I'd swallowed a big rock. My heart sank. I went upstairs, trying not to anticipate what the *news* would be. I went to the bathroom. I put up my unfinished homework. I heard Nick come in downstairs. I fussed with my stuffed animals—stalling. Eventually Ben, Jenny, and I made our way downstairs for the news.

Nick was sitting in the living room. Mom was right beside him. Nick smiled confidently, obviously eager to share the news. "Hey! How you guys doing?! Your mother and I have some special news. We wanted you three to be the first to know."

I dared to look at Ben and Jenny, but their eyes were locked with Nick's in anticipation. I imagined they thought Nick would announce that we were going to Big Surf Waterpark or something. I wasn't so hopeful.

Nick went on. "Your mother is a very special lady. I know how much you love her, and now I have fallen in love with her. I care about her, and I care about the three of you too." He did an exaggerated blink and looked at each one of us with a big smile, revealing his teeth over a cleft chin. There was a separation between his front two upper teeth.

I looked at Mom. She didn't look as confident. In fact, I daresay there was a trace of apology in her eyes. She said nothing. Nick did all the talking. He took her hand in his, smiled at her, then turned back to face us. "I asked your mother to marry me. We got married this weekend." He smiled again.

My mind reeled.

Married? Like, you already GOT married? Nobody asked US? And now Nick is my STEPDAD? This wasn't good news. This was awful.

Nick made great pizza and he made Mom laugh. He played games and was fun.

But NO! This is not good news.

I didn't want him moving into our new home. He wouldn't just be sleeping on the couch either. He would be with Mom, sleeping with her. Mom had a new husband?

There was more. Sometimes, Nick creeped me out. He'd get too close, and he told dirty jokes that made me feel uncomfortable. Other times he would play the "jiggle monster game," pretending to be a wild monster who hunted children. Ben, Jenny, and I would race around the house, hiding and laughing in the thrill of the hunt. If we were caught, he would tickle us as we tried to escape. He would squish us between his legs and jiggle us into uncontrollable laughter. We'd be laughing so hard that I'd try to dismiss the awkwardness of being between his thighs.

I didn't want him to live with us.

Now *he* would be the one making decisions for our family with Mom.

He's the head of our home!

A cold shudder ran through my core. It had only been six months since Mom and Dad's divorce was final.

I was caught up in my own thoughts and then realized Nick said he'd be moving his stuff in next weekend.

Wait! Stop!

Mom looked at us. How do you respond to "good news" that you think is awful? I glossed over my shock by trying to seem interested in details. "So, when did you get married? What church did you go to?"

And why didn't anyone ask us kids?

I tried to smile as Mom explained that they'd gone to the justice of the peace. "Miss Toni and Dan were there as witnesses."

This was the final blow to the end of family as I knew it. We were suddenly a different family, with a new head of household. I looked at Ben and Jenny sitting beside me on the black vinyl love seat. The blank looks on their faces mirrored what I was feeling. They were six and four. They understood even less than I did. All it meant to them was that Nick would move in with a few pieces of furniture.

I was ticked and felt betrayed . . . again. I had to leave. I wanted to run and get far away. Now we were someone else's kids in someone else's house. I looked at the dice clock marking time, hating it.

Stupid clock.

I excused myself. "I better get back to my homework. I've got a lot." That was true, but my mind wasn't on homework. It was on the word *family*. Suddenly, I didn't like that word.

I considered how Mom and Dad had actually given me the choice of who I wanted to live with when they split. I labored considering the choice. I loved them both, but I was a Daddy's girl. I wanted to be with him. But I loved Mom too! How would she feel?

It was right for me to go with Mom. Here I could give my *best*, and be there for Ben and Jenny. Dad would miss us, but Mom needed me.

But now Mom had Nick. Except for Ben and Jenny's sake, I wanted out. The decisions were all made and complete. This was to be our new life. I was mad with no way to express it.

"Child, I am the Head of your forever home."

The Great King swept through the halls of His magnificent kingdom. His booming words echoed as they made their way earthward to bring light to the abyss.

"I exist in a realm crossing all time. One day you will look back and see that I have been walking with you all along, teaching you to walk upright in the face of opposition. I will never leave you or forsake you. I am preparing a place for you even now. You are Mine.

"I am your Father."

By fourth grade my self-esteem had gone from shaky to nonexistent. My handwriting mirrored my identity. It was so small my teacher couldn't read my work. Dad wasn't there to help with homework. I shut down, unmotivated to do schoolwork, much less homework. I felt numb.

I was shocked when, as an adult, I came across my childhood diary.

I could barely read my own writing. It was so small it was barely legible.

Mr. Simpson was my fourth-grade teacher. One day, he had a talk with me. Adjusting his horn-rimmed glasses and giving his bushy moustache a twitch, he said, "You need to try harder, Shelly. Apply yourself." He added the kicker, "You want to pass, don't you?"

I looked at him blankly, nodding my head to appease him.

Pass? Why bother? Who even cares?

He didn't have a clue. And I didn't try any harder.

Mr. Simpson eventually resorted to restricting me from recess every day. Our class ate lunch at our desks. Afterwards, we were dismissed for recess. All the kids would dart for the door, heading outside to the playground, except for me.

All that winter, during every recess I stared at the chalkboard, pretending to be invisible. The room would be utterly quiet except for the distant sounds of my classmates playing outside. The worst part was when the other kids came back in and I was sitting awkwardly alone at my desk.

I wanted to hide.

When Mr. Simpson had had enough eye strain from reading my feeble attempts at schoolwork, he gave me a new seat assignment: a desk wedged between a piano and the blackboard at the front of the class. I was so ashamed. At age eight, going on nine, I knew what it meant to be isolated while at the same time exposed to my peers as a failure. I wanted to disappear entirely.

The Eternal Teacher slowly walked up and down the aisles of the little class-room. He gently touched the head of each child, marveling at His creations. He approached the piano, looking at the teacher.

The child, half-hidden, half-exposed on the other side of the musical instru-ment, drew His attention.

Slowly, tenderly, He knelt beside her. Seeing her shame, He cupped her face in His hands.

"I will remove the bitter taste of this day, but you will not forget. Others taste far more bitterness than this, My child. Recognize them. Love them. And see them how I see you today—precious beyond words."

He studied her face and her heart before blowing a fresh breath of life upon her.

One merciful spring day, we had field day. There were potato sack races, egg tosses, and tug-of-war. The event I remember best was the race around our little gravel field. I put all my shame and frustration into that race. I was outside, and I was *free*.

Mr. Simpson was surely surprised to finally see something in me he could praise. I can still hear him yell, "Go, Shelly! GO!" At that moment something happened. I was probably no faster than the other girls, but I was no longer invisible. Suddenly, I felt *alive*. I had some-thing of worth. I pumped my awkward, skinny legs as fast as I could.

Mr. Simpson had accidentally discovered a key that awoke a sad little girl from the stupor of despondency. If I did my schoolwork, then I could go to recess and use my legs to run. I would play kickball and run. Sometimes I just looked for reasons to run simply because I *could*.

In the motion picture *Chariots of Fire*, Eric Liddell explained his joy of running by saying, "I believe God made me for a purpose, but He also made me fast. And when I run, I feel His pleasure."

Though I am definitely not fast, and I didn't recognize the source at the time, the joy of running became part of me. I could feel the plea-sure of *life* as it coursed through me with the pounding of my heart. Running became a part of my life that would carry me through many difficult seasons yet ahead.

From the banks of the canal on the other side of the wire fence, He savored the scene and relished the sound of the children's shouts and laughter. The sun shone bright and warm, reflecting His pleasure. He gazed upon the awkward girl and saw His breath of life within her.

"Yes, child! That's it. RUN! Feel My life surging through your veins."

He looked to the days ahead, then said, "One day . . . yes, one day, you will run to Me."

That was my last semester at the private school. The repercussions of divorce cut into each area of our lives. Financially, my schooling was too much. I would need to go back to a regular school.

That was a deep cut. The little school had been my last perceived connection to Jesus. There, the teachers told stories of Jesus, and we read verses in the Bible. Jesus was no longer mentioned at home anymore. Even our relationships from church did not withstand the sting, stench, and stain of divorce. Shame cast us out of the church. Leaving the school was yet another costly change.

3

DARK PLACES

*E*ventually, we settled into our new family dynamics. I missed Dad but quickly saw that Mom needed me, maybe more than ever. I began to feel sorry for her as the honeymoon with Nick wore off and his true colors became apparent.

Nick had two sides. There was the side that everyone loved: Nick the storyteller, jokester, and entertaining riddler. He made people laugh and feel comfortable. He was a giver, always wanting to treat people to dinner and events.

Holidays were dynamic. Christmas was Nick's favorite, and he couldn't seem to give enough. The living room floor would be lost beneath a sea of gifts. "Oh! Check that one out over there!" he would joyfully direct. "Open that one!"

Ben would open a gift, maybe a Hot Wheels racetrack or an electric train. Nick would get on the floor, put it together, and play with him for hours.

But for all his fun, charisma, and generosity, Nick also had a dark side. Sometimes he was too personal and touchy-feely. On occasion he would remind me that my body would soon be changing. He would place his hands on me to show and tell me how I would look once I blossomed. He made sure to inform me of other changes as well. I hated how it made me feel.

I tried to reason away the gross feelings that lingered. He wasn't actually doing anything wrong, I told myself. After all, I had clothes on, I rationalized. And I'd always been shy, I convinced myself, so that's probably where the weird feelings were coming from.

This happened more than once in different settings and manners. Sometimes he was more overt than at other times. It was just enough to gross me out and not enough for me to say anything.

Sometimes things happened that were surreal and creepy, like when I woke up to find someone kneeling beside my bed in the middle of the night.

Is someone really here beside the bed? Why would someone be kneeling here on the floor? I was terrified and pulled the sheets over my head.

When it happened again, I sat up in my bed.

"Who's there?" I asked.

I had to know. I could see a figure kneeling beside my bed.

"Mom? Is that you?"

I knew it wasn't Mom, but it felt safer to ask if it was her. *Why would anyone else be there?*

"No, it's me," Nick's voice said nonchalantly. "I was just looking for something. I found it. Go back to sleep."

What was he looking for in the middle of the night beside my bed?

One morning I woke up to find my panties pulled down to my knees. It scared me, so I asked Mom why that would have been. She had no reason to consider anything other than what she told me: "You probably got really hot when you were sleeping."

I knew that wasn't what happened. It didn't match the disturbed feeling that went along with the way I felt when I woke up. I wasn't satisfied with her answer, but it didn't seem worth pursuing either. It was easier just to drop it.

The Great I Am was there. He knew what was happening. He saw it all and winced with grief as the scenes unfolded.

They no longer cried out to Him or thought of Him. They simply carried on.

Another part of Nick was scary in a different way. He would go into periods where his personality seemed to sort of shift. It was frightening because it would happen without warning. Nick would be fun, social, and lively, then suddenly sink into a deep funk.

During those funky periods, he was unpredictable. He would become uncharacteristically quiet and reserved—even pensive—then for no apparent reason he would fly into a raging fit. There was never a clear warning, but during his rants he was confrontational, attacking us verbally with irrational accusations followed by interrogations. It was weird.

He often suspected that someone was purposely messing with him. Something would set him off, agitating or offending him, and he would go on a hunt to find someone to accuse.

One of my first encounters with this behavior was an evening after school when I'd asked if I could go play at the park. Nick nodded. "Be home by six o' clock. We'll eat when your mom gets home." Mom was a real estate agent. That evening she was with a buyer, showing a house.

My friend was at the park, so we swung on the swings, engrossed in talk of school. I checked my watch periodically. When I checked again, it read 5:41—the same time it had ten minutes earlier.

I realized it had stopped working and jumped off the swing. "Oh, shoot!" I cried, running to the clubhouse to check the community clock. It read 6:11. I turned to run home when suddenly I saw Nick marching around the corner. His face was red and his eyes were bulging.

"Who the *hell* do you think you are?" he bellowed.

My friend stood awkwardly watching as I stammered, "I'm . . . I'm sorry. My watch stopped. I just saw that it stopped and went to check the time. Here. Look." I extended my wrist. "I didn't mean—" I tried showing him the watch, but he cut me off, waving his arms.

"Do you take me for some sort of fool?" he screamed. "I told you to be home at six. You get your ass home now!"

I was scared. I didn't know if I should run ahead of him or stay beside him, hoping he'd cool down. I walked quickly, hoping I wouldn't further aggravate him. That time he cooled off. I was grounded for a month.

I'd only heard Mom and Dad argue once. They may have argued more, but if they did, they kept it under wraps. Mom and Nick fought often, and it wasn't hidden.

When Mom and Nick argued, it was terrifying. Nick's voice was full of venom and fury. I remember many nights sitting at the top of the stairs, listening to them argue downstairs in the living room. It broke my heart to hear him yell at Mom in such berating ways. He used words that weren't allowed in our house before, along with other words I'd never heard of.

He was so loud and angry. Mom would be distraught. You could hear them from any room in the house. If Ben and Jenny came out of their rooms, I would let them sit with me for a minute before sending them back to bed.

"It's okay," I'd say reassuringly. "They're just blowing off steam. You better get back in bed though. Don't want to get caught if he comes up here." I was afraid what would happen if Nick came upstairs and found us out of bed, listening to them.

One time, during one of their quarrels, I had to go to the bathroom so bad. There was a pause in their argument, but I was afraid to go pee lest I draw attention to the fact that I was awake. He started yelling again. I should have gone to the bathroom as he yelled, but I wanted to make sure it didn't escalate. By the next pause I couldn't hold it any longer. I tiptoed to the bathroom and lowered myself to the toilet water so I would be silent. Tears fell as I became aware of my pathetic helplessness.

I crept back to the railing at the top of the stairs and sat there till the argument defused, making sure Mom was okay. Their fights usually ended with Mom crying and doors slamming. My inclination was to run and comfort her, but I couldn't. That would infuriate Nick and make matters worse. I had never experienced hate before, but I heard it in Nick and now it was beginning to develop within me. I silently hoped Mom would leave him.

Nick refereed for local athletic teams to earn extra cash. When he and Mom got married, he offered to coach Ben's Little League team. The whole family attended the games. While Nick coached, Mom kept the score sheets. Jenny and I watched. We had fun cheering Ben and his friends from the bleachers.

With each ensuing season, Nick became more critical of Ben. After their games, he made a point of talking about how good the other boys played, while criticizing my brother. As time went on, the pattern continued, and Nick seemed to be stuck in his angst over Ben. Eventually it became the essence of their relationship.

Dear, gentle Ben. He was a good, fun-loving kid with a giant heart. There was no logical reason for Nick to belittle him, but he did—all the time.

When Nick was degrading Mom or Ben, it wasn't safe to come to their defense. It only stirred hostility and backfired on everyone. There was no telling when Nick would be more prone to lose it.

When I was in seventh grade, Nick volunteered to coach a team of older boys. Most of the boys on the team were my classmates. At first I thought it would be cool. It gave me a safe way to get to know the guys better.

One game night, Nick was warming up the team when I stopped to ask him if I could have money to buy a snow cone. "Sure." He reached in his pocket for a dollar. "Just bring me the change."

I bought the snow cone, put the change in my pocket, and started talking with one of the boys on the team, who I had a crush on. He walked with me as I headed toward the dugout to give Nick the change. We talked about an upcoming field day. We were looking forward to the 100-yard dash and the standing long jump. We both had long legs and had a chance at placing.

The next thing I knew, Nick was storming out of the dugout, furious that I had kept the change from the snow cone.

Bewildered at the craziness of what he was saying—and shrinking with embarrassment that this was happening in front of my classmates —I tried to defend myself. "I was on my way to give it to you!" I said.

He edged toward me, nostrils flaring, face red and voice blaring. "You selfish little brat, I gave you money, and what do you do with it? Keep it for yourself?"

I wanted to creep backward, but froze, hoping to avoid any attention.

I clumsily pulled the change out of my pocket. "It's not like that. I just—"

He grabbed my shirt, thrusting me against the chain link fence near the dugout. Heads turned our way. Sweat rolled down his face, red with anger. I wanted to crawl under the bleachers.

Everyone can see!

It was times like these that Nick seemed to be an entirely different person. He actually looked different—especially his eyes. You didn't want to look at them because they were so menacing, but when you did, it was as if he'd cashed out and someone else was in in his body. It was scary.

Todd, the boy I'd been talking and flirting with, dared to jump in. "Coach, uh, sir, please. I—" Suddenly, Nick snapped back, aware of his surroundings and the onlookers obviously ready to jump in if the scene were to escalate.

He glanced at the other coaches, then back at me, "Go sit with your mother, and don't get up till the game is over. We'll discuss this at home." He turned to Todd and scowled, "Why aren't you warming up? Get back out, and I'll decide whether or not you play this game."

Fortunately, by the time we got home, he'd gotten a grip on his emotions and saved face by once again giving me consequences for disrespecting him.

That was a typical scene. Scenes played out in different ways on different occasions. No one in the immediate family was immune from Nick's unprompted lashings. His rants were always accompanied by the same signs: veins bulging on his temples, eyes racing, chest bowed, face red.

He never did more than push or shove. It was the ungrounded accusations and threats that kept us wary. In time we learned to manage and tried to stay out of the way when he went into a funk.

Nick's erratic behavior was like that of an alcoholic, only Nick didn't drink and anything could trigger him. In fact, it would have at least explained things if he *did* drink. Instead we tiptoed through life as if it were a minefield, feeling like we were part of the problem. We had to be careful what we did or didn't do, hoping to not set off an explosion.

Though he couldn't control the outbursts of his mental and emotional roller-coaster rides, I think he actually exercised a lot of restraint in not letting loose on us physically. Even so, the intensity of his rants increased with time. We didn't know any better than to accept things as they were. Mom was too worn down to do more than cope. Nick crushed her over and over with berating comments. That devastated me, and I saw that it broke her already bruised heart.

More than ever I felt responsible for Ben and Jenny. Nick's aversion to Ben was hard to ignore. Maybe it was because Ben was more representative of Dad. Whatever it was, Nick picked on him all the time.

It bothered me that I could never make up for Nick's lashes on Ben's young ego. The best I could do was step in whenever possible to buffer Ben during Nick's tirades. A timid, skinny girl, I was no match for Nick. My best efforts were to try to interrupt his thought process. I learned that he responded and cooled off if I showed respect without bowing down. I became adept at changing the direction of the conversation with enthusiasm and purposed cheerfulness. "Hey . . . so, are we gonna make caffe latte? How much milk do we need?"

One constant that I look back on with great appreciation were times spent with Miss Toni's family. Our families would celebrate holidays and special occasions together. Miss Toni was always there—a friend to Mom and us kids. I knew she built Mom up every time Nick tore her down. That relationship would prove to be a thread that withstood time and heartaches over the years.

They didn't look to Him, nor did they hear His words.

"Come back! I have so much more for you." The Shepherd watched longingly. He knew things would get worse before they got better.

He looked at the girl striving to make peace and said, "These dark days will become your former days. It will get darker, but I am watching over you. I will see you through and turn your mourning to laughter."

That was the year Dad became serious with Miss Ellie. They had been dating for months when Dad introduced us. Mom had actually worked with Miss Ellie at the realty office. She was pretty although she and Mom looked nothing alike. She had olive skin, soft-brown eyes, short brown hair, and a healthy, athletic frame. She was quick-witted and had a wry sense of humor.

I liked her but was less than optimistic after seeing what had happened with Mom and Nick.

Soon we began to share weekend time with them together. It hurt. We didn't have much time with Dad, and now it, too, was to be shared.

I knew he loved us, but that sacred "Dad time" was fading away. We weren't going to be the special ones in his life, as we had been.

Before long Dad was telling us they would be getting married. My heart sank. I wanted to be happy that Dad wouldn't be lonely now. Miss Ellie seemed like a good lady, but I'd already learned that a new husband or wife meant that kids took a backseat role in family dynamics.

I saw it with Nick. He had his own kids from a previous marriage. Though he would talk about his kids, he seldom saw them.

Miss Ellie was a few years younger and didn't have kids. I knew she would want her own children—not somebody else's.

Once they got married, Dad and Miss Ellie began their new life. They bought a new home. We kids would still be loved, but our importance shrank yet again.

When Mom and Dad each remarried, their new spouses became their first love. The simple truth was that the spouses themselves had no natural affection for us. They'd fallen in love with my parents. Ben, Jenny, and I were just part of the package.

I saw us kids as burdens, and that made me want to apologize to Miss Ellie. I could understand how it might be frustrating to watch a portion of the family income go out every month for three kids who belonged to another woman.

I also understood that Miss Ellie had not seen our first steps or heard our first words, nor was she there when our lives were split down the middle. We weren't endeared to her.

Miss Ellie hadn't been a mom yet, so how would she understand that our hearts and identities were broken and bruised—that everything in us wanted to cleave to the one person who was our forever champion?

I wasn't intellectually gifted, but I was overly conscientious. I knew it would have been easier for Nick and Miss Ellie if we kids weren't part of the deal. No one ever implied that, but I believed it.

Either house we went to, we were always somebody else's kids. I hated it.

In the deep recesses of my mind, these and other thoughts wove their way into who I was becoming.

I remembered how I'd been taught to give my best, and how I'd failed. Now my "best" was my family. I didn't want to share Mom or Dad any more than I knew Miss Ellie or Nick wanted to have to share them with us.

Why do I have to give my Mom and my Dad? Aren't they mine?

Secretly, in my childish ignorance, I considered this my punishment for having a heart that only gave second best, as I had with the Lucy doll. To this end I felt that I had failed God again.

I saw myself as a beat-up piece of lost luggage, filled with stinky old clothes that reeked. I was full of anger, disappointment, rejection, and failure. More than anything, I felt unwanted.

The heavenly Father tucked the girl in with grace and an unperceived kiss as she cried herself to sleep once more. He saw every dark and weighty part of her, but He saw more than what she saw.

"You are Mine. I am your Father. I watched your first footsteps. I see your

beating heart. I know your thoughts. I can't wait for you to know My thoughts. I will remove the darkness and fill you with good things."

4

GOODBYE TO INNOCENCE

*I*t was June 1980 when I stepped into my eighth-grade graduation processional. I caught my reflection in the cafeteria window.

I hope Dad sees how grown-up I look.

I was wearing my first pair of high-heeled shoes, though I could barely walk in them.

Inside the cafeteria, the noise of the crowd rose. Family and friends were packed into the air-conditioned room, which was bright with fluorescent light. I looked around, hoping to spot Dad.

Okay. There's Mom and Nick. Maybe Dad's running late.

It was only eighth grade, but it was a formal ceremony. After the presentation, friends and family mingled, taking photos, eating cookies, and drinking punch. I surveyed the crowd once more. No sign of Dad.

A lump rose in my throat.

Where is he?

Jenny snuck up behind me and pinched my waist playfully. She had a ribbon in her hair and crumbs on her cheek. Her athletic body looked pretty in her new dress. She extended a cookie. "Mmm.

Cookies are good. Want one?" Another Instamatic camera flashed. I stopped searching the room, my heart broken.

Ben nudged his way through the crowd, obviously uncomfortable, wearing a collared shirt and slacks. He was looking for his friend John. John's cousin was graduating too. Mom and Nick followed behind Ben. I could see they were proud of me.

Isn't that enough?

In the midst of the crowd, The King weaved among His favorite creations. He weighed their thoughts and emotions: joy, boredom, pride, hunger, disappointment, anticipation.

He marveled at their unique differences, appreciating the work of His hands. He was aware of every hidden thought and emotion. "They always move to the next activity without really appreciating the moment they're in," He mused.

He noticed the girl was looking for her dad. She looked grown-up and more like her grandmother every day.

He saw her hidden tears as she knelt and pretended to fix her shoe strap, hoping no one would see how hurt and disappointed she felt.

The next day was Saturday. Saturdays were my "van day." Nick had offered to help pay for my plane ticket to go see relatives in St. Louis if I would wash the van each week for a year.

This was a nine-passenger Chevy van. Nick ran a carpool, driving the three-hour, round-trip trek each day through the dusty desert back and forth to Palo Verde nuclear plant.

I had to use a step ladder to access the top of the van. Nick reminded me, "I'm going to inspect it roof to tires." And he did, too. But I never had to do anything twice, having learned how to do it right the first time. I took pride knowing I did a good job upholding my end of the deal.

It was early June and the afternoon sun was hot. After finishing the van, I was sweaty and dirty. I'd shower before we went to Miss Toni and Dan's for a barbecue. I put up the bucket and soap then threw towels in the laundry.

I wish Mike didn't have to go out of town. We should be having fun celebrating graduation.

Mike had been my boyfriend throughout eighth grade. In reality, he was a dear friend and buffer to Nick's funks, tirades, and creepiness.

Ben was with John, and Jenny was out bike riding. Mom was still at work. I was about to take a shower.

Ugh. No shampoo again.

We were down to one bottle. It would be in Mom's shower. I wrapped a towel around me and walked across the living room, where Nick was watching TV. He mumbled. "What ya doin'? Thought you already showered."

I had earlier that morning. "Yeah, I did. But I'm all gross now. Just washed the van. Remember?"

I grabbed the Suave and headed back to the bathroom, suddenly uncomfortable to be wearing just a towel. Back in my bathroom, I examined my hair. I really didn't want to wash it again. I'd just washed it the day before, and it always looked better the day after anyway.

I took my towel off and put on a shower cap. Suddenly, Nick was at the bathroom door. No. Nick was now on *my side* of the door.

He closed it behind him.

I froze. The towel was steps away, lying on the floor next to him.

I looked at my clean clothes on the counter and my dirty ones on the floor, willing them to be on me. But instead . . .

It wasn't rape. In fact, he didn't even reveal himself. He said it was just a game. It was only . . .

It was WRONG. And it was gross, and it made me feel dirty.

And God?! All-knowing, all-present, He *was there*. He could have stepped out from behind that hidden veil of eternity. But He didn't.

And how many worse things happen all the time? And why doesn't He stop them? Could I have stopped it? Why didn't I say anything to make him stop?

I was shocked, ashamed, disgusted, confused, and afraid. I was not only weak; now I was dirty.

He saw her skin crawl and her heart freeze.

"Breathe, child, breathe. I am here."

She was unable to bear His voice. It was too much to consider that He was there . . . and that He didn't stop it.

He saw the man's conflict: The man embraced his sin nature, willingly crossing boundaries and inflicting great hurt. The man also was sickened at what took place. Then lies and excuses quickly took over his thoughts, and soon he was denying that he'd done anything wrong at all.

The Father bowed His beautiful crown of glory in grief and cried. Then He lifted His head and watched from the other side of the veil. It was painful to see. She was His child.

The man was not a dark and sinister stranger. He was His creation too. One sinner among many, giving himself over to a weak and fallen nature, as each eventually did in his or her own unique way.

It pained Him every time, taking Him to the same point:

To the point of nails driven into flesh, lungs gasping for air . . .

To the point of His Son for their sin.

I don't remember much from Miss Toni's barbecue that night except walking around numbly, ashamed, wanting only to be alone.

The next morning in our kitchen, Mom asked me, "You all right?"

I avoided her eyes, busying my hands with whatever was within arm's reach. I picked up a towel and dried dishes. She pressed the question again. "Shelly, something's not right. What's going on?"

I masked it. "Dad didn't even come. It was my graduation." That was true. It really hurt.

She picked up an ashtray and emptied it in the trash. She and Nick both smoked. Most of the adults I knew smoked.

"You know he loves you," she said. "I'm sure he had a good reason."

It was a feeble excuse and I saw it on her face.

"Sure, Mom." I said without any emotion.

Maybe I could just slip the other thing into the conversation.

"Mom, do you think you could maybe say something to Nick?"

"About your Dad?" Her puzzled look revealed that she didn't have a clue.

The hem on my T-shirt had come undone. I messed with it, avoiding her eyes. Would she *hear* me?

I took the chance. "No, Nick . . . he has this game. I don't want him to play it again, and I'm afraid he'll get really mad if I talk about it."

My chest tightened with fear. I could hardly breathe.

Oh my gosh. It doesn't matter what she says to him. He's gonna know I told.

"Wait. No . . . Never mind, Mom. Just forget about it."

There was no turning back. Her faced paled and she half fell, half sat down in a chair. "Shelly, what are you talking about?"

I replayed the scene in my mind, describing it for her, trembling as I did. Her face went blank. "Shelly, it's good that you told me. I'm glad you did."

How would *he* respond? At least it was out. Mom assured me she'd talk to him, soon. She rose from her seat slowly. I could see she was pondering her next steps. Then she looked at me and said, "This won't happen again."

Mine was the room farthest from theirs, but I heard everything that night. Nick was ranting and cursing. "That conniving little . . . I ought to go in there and kick her ass!"

I lay frozen in bed, wondering if I would wake up in the morning. During the rages I always wondered just how far Nick might actually take things if he were really pushed. He was being pushed.

Finally, a door slammed and the ranting stopped. I traced the outline of the Palo Verde tree shadowing against my window. Waiting.

I clutched a necklace beneath my pillow. It was a cross pendant Mom had given me. I hoped that if I didn't make it to morning, perhaps holding on to the cross would somehow help me get to heaven.

Now I lay me down to sleep, I pray the Lord my soul to keep. If I should die before I wake, I pray the Lord my soul to take.

Nick never came in, and eventually I fell asleep.

The Protector kept watch through the night. He whispered sleep upon the girl to carry her to morning. He would not intervene beyond the hidden veil, nor would He ever leave.

The next day Mom found a place for us at a women's shelter. I was grateful that Mom had taken action. It meant a lot that she acknowledged that what Nick had done was wrong. She heard me. She believed me. She did something about it.

Nick was arrested. He gave a full confession and went to jail. Mom posted bail, and a restraining order prohibited him from seeing me before the pending trial. Even so, I was glad to be in a place he didn't know.

The shelter was far from our house. We shared a room with two other women and their children. The first thing we did was get our heads washed for lice. I felt dirty with shame.

I didn't know what to tell my friends, so I just made up things when I used the pay phone to call them. They would know something was wrong eventually, when no one answered our home phone.

I longed for the easy company of my best friend, Mike. I wanted to be away from the strangeness of the shelter, the pit I was in, and the darkness that crowded in around me.

It bothered me that Ben and Jenny were being punished because I had told what happened. I felt alone, ashamed, and guilty.

Dad and Miss Ellie lived close to where we lived. I waited for Dad, my hero, to come and take us out of the craziness. Dad wouldn't want us to stay at the shelter. He would take us to live with him. I knew there was room in his house for us. It was a safe place.

It didn't happen.

A large part was probably because Miss Ellie was pregnant and close to her due date. We kids would be more than added occupants. We came with heavy issues. It was probably not the best arrangement for a new baby. Still, there were two empty rooms in addition to the baby's room. I was crushed.

That same month, Dad's brother got married and the reception was to be at Dad's house. A friend drove us to the wedding, hoping it would lift our spirits. It was nice to dress up and get a break from the shelter. I did pretty well getting through the wedding. I couldn't be a baby. What would Ben and Jenny think? I needed to be a good example. I put on smiles and made polite conversation.

By the time we got to the reception, I couldn't keep up the act any longer. It hurt to see Dad laughing, being a good host, seemingly oblivious to me. In retrospect I knew he simply didn't know what to do.

Shame and rejection weighed heavy on me. There was nowhere to run. I thought of the empty bedrooms in the back of the house and found refuge in one of the closets. I sat on my haunches—invisible—

choking on tears, feeling dirty and abandoned. Where else could I go?

I was confused. Dad had always protected me before. He had shown me tenderness and cradled me in his arms. He taught me love. Why didn't Dad take me in his arms and tell me he was sorry all of this had happened to his girl?

I longed to hear him tell me I would be okay, that it was over. But it wasn't. That's not what happened.

In the dark, lonely closet, the King grieved with his daughter. Tears soaked His garment as He tucked her close in His mighty arms. He spoke words of promise and hope though she wouldn't hear those words for years.

"Child, you will see Me," He said.

With each tear came another stroke of that magnificent balm — grace.

He watched the child's earthly father nurse his own wounded heart. He heard his silent prayers and saw his hidden tears.

"Yes, son," the King responded to the pleas of the broken man. "Yes, I will take care of her."

The time at the women's shelter seemed long although it was only five or six weeks. A court date was set, and we moved back home. Nick stayed in a hotel until the day of our trial. Mom reassured me Nick was not hostile toward me. I wasn't so sure.

Time passed more quickly when I landed a job with the City of Phoenix Youth Employment Program. All summer Mom drove me downtown to the Department of Economic Security. I ran back and forth from the DES offices to city hall, making copies of landmark cases, filing, and learning how to check records on microfiche. It was a great way to keep my thoughts occupied and productive in a neutral, safe environment.

I remembered the angry words Nick had shouted to Mom on the night I'd told on him. "This is nothing but a ploy to break up our marriage, Merry," he had yelled. "Don't you see it?"

If only I were so smart. If only I had just made it up.

The time at the shelter was not pleasant, but the time away from Nick was calm and free of drama. Even though I could see the pain in Mom's eyes, the absence of Nick's presence provided a reprieve. It was as though we could breathe and didn't have to worry about setting off a landmine.

The big day finally came. Our case was to go to trial before a judge.

"This is not a big deal," a woman from Child Protective Services told me with a smile. "You don't have to worry. You'll just go in and talk to the judge. It won't take long at all. You may not even have to say anything." She was trying to keep things light, but her reassurances didn't lessen the heavy weight that was crushing me.

The room was cold and stagnant as we waited. I knew our future was on the line. Nick had signed his confession without contesting. He would do time. It was a slam dunk case for the state.

I was told what was at stake. Nick would lose his job. We'd have to sell the house, move, change schools, and make new friends.

Before we went in to see the judge, Nick's lawyer asked to talk with Mom and then me. Again, I felt alone and ill-equipped to make these decisions.

The woman from CPS assured me I didn't have to speak with him if I didn't want to, so Mom talked to him. I remember that he kept talking to her about our family being kept together.

That was my deal breaker. Maybe there was another way to work this out—a way that wouldn't destroy Ben's and Jenny's lives too.

"Do you really want to go through with this?" the attorney asked.

Seriously? I didn't want a part of any of this in the first place!

"You could drop charges if he agrees to go to counseling," another adult pointed out.

I really just want to run.

We camped out on this idea for a few minutes. I listened to their reasoning.

Then I heard someone counter, "But then again, if you force someone to go to counseling, will they really get anything out of it?"

I want my Dad!

It didn't occur to me that he'd had the option to be there.

"What if we just agreed to work things out?" someone else proposed.

I looked at them; they were each waiting for my answer. These were adults. I was the child. They were all waiting on me.

Don't they know the right thing to do?

There were three of them. One sounded convincing, another seemed frustrated. A third seemed to be pleading with me with silent, guilty eyes. To do what, I had no idea.

Will the real adult please step forward and HELP me?!

Was this really happening?

It felt like a scene from a movie, only this was real life, my life, and it stung. I was being asked to make the decision. Me. Not my mom. Not the attorneys. Not the judge.

I made the best decision I could, based on what I considered would be best for my brother and sister.

Maybe this is giving my best.

Charges were dropped. Within a day or two the restraining order was lifted. It was as if nothing had ever happened. We picked up right where we left off.

I saw Mike again, but everything *had* changed. He was the same, but *we* were strangers now. He was still innocent. I was damaged and had grown up in ways he couldn't understand.

At thirteen, I'd learned to work a forty-hour-a-week job. I knew what it meant to make choices for others over self. I'd learned things about people I didn't want to know. I'd said goodbye to innocence.

He stormed through the halls into the wings of the courtroom.

The Great Judge looked at their faces and studied their thoughts.

"Fools! Justice is not a game or a market with bargaining chips. You play at justice, righteousness, mercy, grace . . ."

He shook with holy indignation, "Mine is the only standard of right and wrong." He turned His face from them.

"I work righteousness and justice for the oppressed. My ways alone will prevail."

He looked to the girl. It was time. She would need to walk her own walk with Him.

"Your garments are torn and stained, but I'm giving you new clothes. I am adorning you with the elegance of humility. It's entwined with cords of My love. You'll see once you let go of the shame that is not yours to wear."

The Great I AM issued an invitation addressed with her name. "But you must rise and turn to Me. Child, I want your best; I want your heart."

5

THE BOOK

*F*all began a new season of life for my family. Miss Ellie gave birth to my new sister, Christine. She would have the best dad. I knew Dad would love her well.

I also knew things would change more for Ben, Jenny, and me. I couldn't help but think this meant the end of us as Dad's kids. Now we were his *other* kids. I didn't dislike this new baby, but I concluded she would always have a more prominent place in Dad's heart. She would be his front and center. We would be peripheral. Dad's new family was now complete.

I entered my freshman year of high school hoping for my own new beginnings. I had taken modeling classes the year before as a gift from Mom and Nick. The money I earned from the summer job was enough to pay for professional photos to start a portfolio. In the fall I signed on with a talent agency and finally felt like my life was taking a turn for the better.

My first professional job was to fly with a group of college students to the Grand Canyon for an NCAA sportswear shoot. The media crew bought our tickets for the small private plane, food, and lodging. They only paid traveling expenses for the models, so Mom permitted me to go under the care of one of the video crew moms.

The first day was a photo shoot in the woods along the rim of the Grand Canyon. On the second day, two of us were instructed to hike a mile-and-a-half to a spot on the trail down the canyon, then wait to hear "Go!" from our walkie talkie. We'd run fifty yards and start over. It was ADVENTURE. It had been too long since I'd been on an adventure. Here I was . . . away, free, and exploring new opportunities. It was a blast. I considered that maybe I had *something* of value.

The modeling jobs were intermittent, but the pay was great. The spontaneity and variety of it was exciting. There were photo shoots, commercials, and a couple of runway jobs. I met modeling industry executive Eileen Ford and dreamed of one day visiting her again at her New York agency. It was a lofty dream, but it had me looking forward.

Mom was my biggest support, always taking me on interviews, to auditions, and to jobs until I could drive on my own. She believed in me even if I didn't. "You can do this, Shelly. There are no limits for you." She helped me believe that maybe I really could.

Even so, I didn't see myself as pretty. I knew I had the "girl next door" look. The value was that I looked like every other girl, and marketers liked that.

When kids at school heard I was a model, I found more acceptance. The attention was great, but I made sure not to get close with anyone except a few safe friends.

As exciting as it was, I felt phony. People saw something on the outside, and I saw something entirely different on the inside. I was convinced that if anyone knew what was really beneath the "pretty" surface, they would see the ugly truth. They'd see me in all my shame, challenges, and pathetic weakness.

One day as I was running, my thoughts trailed to the book I was reading. The main character was a lady who was in a ski accident and her face had to be reconstructed.

The only value I perceived I had was "face" value. *If something like that ever happened to me, I would be back wedged between the blackboard and the piano. A misfit of no use or worth to anyone.*

Fear was always at my heels.

Fear was at my heels, but *the King* was right before me. Still, I was not aware of Him.

"Child, have you not heard Me? I designed you.

"I am forging you for beauty from the inside out.

"Your scars will become My beauty marks of redemption.

"Your appearance does not give you your value. I will give you true beauty for ashes.

"Accept My invitation."

That fall I made friends with a girl in biology class named Julie. She invited me to something she called "the Harvest." The Harvest was a midweek service just for youth at Julie's church. I liked Julie, so I thought I'd give it a try.

It had been years since I'd set foot in a church, and the Harvest was much bigger than the group my parents had led. It was a new place, with people I didn't know, but strangely, I felt at home. It was safe.

I continued to go each week even if Julie didn't. The messages about the Father in heaven stirred something up inside of me. I was like a hungry orphan standing outside of a bakery, savoring the aromas, longing for more. By summer break I'd made a few more friends.

There was an older classman, Chip, whose girlfriend, Michelle, went to my school. He was our group leader at the Harvest. Once I settled into the group, Chip began asking me questions. "Shelly, do you believe these stories?"

I'd been taught stories about Jesus, but no one had ever asked me if I *believed* the stories. Of course I did . . . Didn't I?

The next week he had another question. "Shelly, do you know what Jesus did for you at the cross?"

What's with this guy and all his questions?

"Yeah, He died on the cross. Chip, I grew up in the church when I was little. We stopped going when Mom and Dad divorced. I know the stories." I had missed hearing the stories and opening my Bible. I recalled how we used to pray. I missed that too, but I wasn't going to explain all that to Chip. Instead, I said, "Why do you keep asking?"

"I guess because I care," Chip said with a shrug. The church building was closing for the evening, so Chip asked if we could go somewhere and talk more. He smiled and assured me, "I think you'll want to hear what I have to share."

Michelle was standing beside him. "It's cool. He really knows a lot about the Bible." I looked at them both and saw their sincerity.

"Okay, sure."

We all went to my house and sat out on the front patio. The night was warm, the sky was clear, and the moon was high. The neighborhood was quiet except for the three of us.

We talked a few minutes about the summer camp coming up. Then Chip started in with the questions again.

He always had a smile on his face and was not a pushy person, but his next question surprised me.

"Shelly, do you see yourself as sinner?"

Wow. Really? I knew I messed up a lot, but I really tried to do right by others. I wasn't a troublemaker. In fact, I strived to be a peacemaker. "That's a little harsh, isn't it?" I said a little defensively. "Did I do something wrong?"

He smiled again. There was nothing confrontational in his voice.

"No. But it's important to acknowledge your sin. Our sin is what separates us from God and heaven."

He opened his Bible and had me read these words: "For the wages of sin is death, but the free gift of God is eternal life in Christ Jesus our Lord" (Romans 6:23).

"Shelly, it's not enough to know *about* God," he said, "You could never do enough good things to pay for your sin. The payment for sin is blood."

He went on to explain that Jesus took all sin on Himself. He allowed sin to be placed on Himself just as He allowed Himself to be nailed on the cross. Chip used plain words. "God sent Jesus as a gift to pay for your sins," he said. "He paid the price of *all* sin."

Dad had explained this to me as a young child, but so much had been lost when we suddenly stopped being part of the church. Hearing it again now was different. I was older, and now it was strangely clearer.

Chip went on. "He is both God and man. He had to make the payment with His life in the form of man to satisfy His own holy requirement. In fact, that is the only way you can get to heaven: by believing in Christ and giving your heart to Him."

Next he had me read John 14:6, "I am the way, and the truth, and the life; no one comes to the Father but through Me."

Chip was a really nice guy. He was always drawing people in, making them laugh and helping them feel at home. But now, as he spoke about God, he spoke with power and authority. He believed what he was saying—and I was getting it.

"Chip, you're saying I can know for certain that one day I can be in heaven?"

The three of us were sitting on boulders that bordered the patio. Chip couldn't sit still any longer. He stood up excitedly. "Yes!" He looked at Michelle, who was smiling now too. "Shelly, we've been praying for you."

Chip looked at me to make sure I was tracking with him. "Here's the deal: God wants your name in the Lamb's Book of Life. God gave His best. He sent His Son to pay the price so your name could be written in that book. One day you can stand before Him as He opens the book and reads your name there."

He paused again. I could tell he was choosing his words carefully. "You have to believe it and *receive* it as a gift. God wants to give you eternal life starting now. But you have to accept the gift. You have to say yes and take it."

I was stunned. I knew the stories. We had been deeply involved in the church. Now here was this guy telling me I could know for sure that God had made a way for me to be with Him in heaven. I could say yes and receive His promise of eternal life and know that one day I'd be there with Him. I didn't have to earn my way there.

I had been so burdened by not having given my best that I had not considered the need to *receive* God's best. This was the most amazing thing I'd ever heard.

"Okay," I said, "so what do I do now?"

Chip and Michelle prayed with me. It went something like this:

> *Thank You, God, for sending Jesus.*
> *I know that I sin, and I'm sorry.*
> *Jesus, I believe You are God's Son and that You died on the*
> *   cross to pay for my sins. Thank You.*
> *I believe that You rose again from the dead and proved You are*
> *   God's son.*
> *I want my name to be written in Your Book of Life!*
> *I want You to be part of my life.*

We talked a little more. Before Chip and Michelle left, they invited me to start coming to the regular services on Sunday morning, adding that I also might want to consider joining a discipleship group.

It was close to midnight when I watched their taillights drive down the street. I remember the overwhelming excitement of knowing for certain that one day I would be in heaven. I didn't have to wonder about it anymore.

The Savior sat on the large stone, enjoying the purity of the night's exchange. Tucked in His arms was an old and heavy book with pages full of names written in blood.

As the conversation between the teenagers continued, He poured out His Spirit and drank in their delight of Him. He had seen this night from a far distance.

He smiled.

Now the girl had a glimpse of what He had for her. It was a small seed, but one day it would crack open and take root to grow.

"I have two books," He said to her. "One is for Me. The other is for you. Read My book, listen for My voice. Ah, I have so much to show you, child!

"But be very careful. You must grow roots. You will face more opposition. There are birds that will try to steal away the seed, and weeds that will get in the way as it begins to grow. The stumbling stones of your life will be a challenge."

I was in a bit of a daze for weeks, processing what the God of heaven and earth had done to make sure we could have a place with Him in heaven. I had a *future!*

God was in heaven, and He knew my name. He'd given me an invitation, signed in His blood—and I'd accepted. My name was in the Lamb's Book of Life.

Soon after that night, my sophomore year started. I signed up for cross-country. I had run only short dashes before, but now I would learn to run distance. I had to teach my body new things, like slowing down, maintaining cadence, form, and proper breathing. It was awkward to begin with. In fact, it was like learning to run all over again. Fortunately, I caught that quicker than I did schoolwork.

Though I grew as a runner, I didn't grow with Christ. I didn't take time to foster a relationship with Him.

Growing with Christ would also mean slowing down, learning cadence, form, and proper breathing—the breath of life by prayer. I didn't recognize that until much later. Chip had planted some amazing "God seed," but it would be years before it actually took root and bore fruit.

I had my church friends, and we continued our Wednesday nights. I even went Sundays, but I didn't get into the Word and didn't grow as a believer.

Life at home hadn't changed either. Nick did not do anything else to me physically, but his mental and emotional blow-ups continued. Sometimes it made me feel like I was crazy.

One afternoon Ben was watching TV, Jenny was making a sandwich, and I was working on homework. All of a sudden, Nick was yelling for us to "get in here now!"

He was in his and Mom's room. "Who took my phone apart? And what did you do with it?" he yelled. He was holding the phone.

We looked at one another dumbfounded as he continued. "Who took the missing piece?" I didn't even know you could unscrew the hand set. Nick was livid. "*What* do you think you're pulling over on me?" We were standing side by side as he stared each of us down to find evidence of guilt. His eyes were menacing and full of accusation. He paced for a minute.

We were teenagers now, and it seemed ridiculous to be interrogated for childish pranks we knew better than to do. Even so, I felt my hands getting sweaty with nervous anxiety.

"What a *rotten* thing to do. I can't believe one of you would do this!" He scowled again, looking for a response. "It's better to tell me now." We were silent. There was nothing to do but stand there frozen.

I racked my brains and began to question myself.

Did I do it?

I knew neither Ben nor Jenny would dare do such a thing.

This had to be a setup to see who would take the fall.

If it was, I wasn't going for it. I was done with his stupid games.

He stopped pacing. "Okay, fine. That's the way you want to play?" He cast another accusing sweep over us. "You're all grounded until you confess. No TV, no phone, and no outings with friends. You go to school and you come straight home." He was done. "Get outta here! I hope you feel good about it."

Part of me wished I had been smart and bold enough to do the deed.

We were perplexed but not surprised. Later, when Nick was gone, we quizzed each other. "What was that all about? You didn't do it, did you?" None of us suspected the other. No. No one had dared, but we all wished we had. We just chalked it up to his strange norm.

The next day Jenny was dusting, doing her chores. She found the missing phone piece on Al's dresser. She took it to Mom, asking her if it was the piece Nick had been looking for. It was. He never mentioned it again, and discreetly, Mom lifted our grounding.

We all had our own ways to cope with Nick. I kept busy, Ben spent time with his friend John, and Jenny was busy excelling at anything she set her hands to. Mom did her best to stand in the way to cover for us when she could see a funk coming on. Usually, though, there was no warning.

As I neared the end of high school, I realized I wouldn't always be in this crazy house. Ben and Jenny were becoming more independent as well. They wouldn't be far behind. I began to look forward to life after high school.

It's only right to acknowledge, there were many good times in those years too. I know Nick cared about us despite his random tirades. We did a lot together as a family, and Nick made sure it would be fun for everyone.

One year Nick bought a boat. During summer break we'd spend weekends out on the lake, skiing and camping. Miss Toni, Dan and their girls spent Thanksgiving with us on Lake Havasu. The holiday dinner was so bad we laughed our way through one dish after the other. Those were good times.

And we were encouraged to bring friends. Often Ben's friend John would come with us on campouts and weekend excursions.

Another year Nick had a pool put in the backyard. He made us laugh and he did provide for us. Looking back on those dark years, I also find good memories.

The Ancient One cast His eyes upon the disjointed family. They were so much like His beloved, Israel.

He looked at His Son, the Great King, who had been pierced for their transgressions, crushed for their iniquities, chastened for their well being and scourged so that they might be healed.

He looked at His children, still lost and wandering.

The older girl had been so close.

"Turn to Me!" He said to them. "See with My eyes. Perceive with My heart. I will give you compassion to overcome all things. Though your hearts break and melt, let Me have them! I will fashion them into something extraordinary! Listen to My Words; I have promises and secrets to share—great treasures ready to be found.

"But you will choose your ways. Your hearts will remain cold and stagnant. You will walk with pain and sorrow and seek earthly satisfactions until you find them to be like dirt in your mouth.

"When your hunger becomes desperation, you will turn. And then, finally in your grief, you will find Me.

"I will be here."

I finally made it to high school graduation. There was never a consideration of not completing high school, but when I finally completed my last tests, I was amazed I had actually finished. I made it to the end. Though it was a huge deal for me privately, I really wanted to skip the whole celebration entirely.

The ceremony was a long, formal presentation. I didn't have any special accomplishments or awards, and no one had any idea what an enormous feat it was for me to be graduating. After all those years, this was it. The school scene had never become my deal; it was a relief simply to be done.

Mom, Nick, Ben, and Jenny came up afterward and gave me hugs. We would meet back at home. Mom had made a cake. It touched me that she was proud, though I suspected she never knew the depth of my scholastic struggle. I was secretly proud of how well I'd hidden it, despite the shame.

Dan and Toni and the girls would be there too. I opted out of the senior trip, as most of my friends had graduated the year before. A gathering with Mom's cake, Grandpa Portillo, and family friends would make for a good celebration.

I said goodbye and congratulations to a few friends before heading to the parking lot. Taking off the bright gold graduation gown, I crossed the field. I heard the rowdy football players heckling one another, and others shouting directions for various parties. I wouldn't miss the high school scene at all.

A man walked in my direction looking out of place. He was alone.

He looks like Dad.

I snatched a glance again, determining not to let false hope rise.

That's MY Dad!

My heart leapt in my chest as I recognized his endearing sideways smile.

Dad came to see me!

Dad was standing before me, congratulating me. "Way to go, kid. I'm proud of you." Those words from my dad were the best words of the night—the most inspiring words I would remember of my graduation.

Father watched the two. It was humorous to see the hearts racing in both of their chests as they attempted to look casual and unmoved by the event.

This was a challenge for the man. The Father understood, though the girl did not. She knew little of her father's story, or the weight of the burdens he still carried.

The Ancient Father was pleased. As they parted, He sealed the memory in the daughter's mind with words of truth, "Your father loves you."

He cherished the moment with them and tucked it in the banks of the girl's prized memories. She would retrieve it many times to savor in years to come.

6

SOMEONE TO WALK WITH

Neither Mom nor Dad ever really talked about college. Neither had done more than take some classes at the local community college. There had been no college plans or funds; and with my academic challenges, I was not scholastically motivated. I lacked vision.

Instead of school, I landed in the arms of a young man named Brad. Brad was a regular customer at the video store where I worked.

Everyone knew and liked Brad—except me. He was attractive, but he wasn't my type. Brad was a cocky bad boy with a take-it-or-leave-it attitude and a strut in his walk. He was too confident in himself for my taste. I was not part of the Brad fan club and was surprised when he asked me out. Strangely, I accepted. It was more as a curious challenge, but I soon recognized I was secretly drawn to his bad boy swank.

Brad wasn't needy. He didn't need me take care of him or protect him or tiptoe around. He was calm, cool, and collected and irresistibly *stable*.

He was strong and lean with crystal blue eyes. Brad's blond hair was cut tight, revealing a strong, tanned neck. I was physically attracted to him, and, happily, I found it was mutual.

The more we hung out around each other, the more I liked him. I felt at ease whenever we were together. Brad was a welcome relief to the emotional roller coaster I was used to.

Since he was a bad boy, I wasn't afraid I would spoil him with my own dirty stains. What you saw with Brad was what you got. What Brad wanted was me—just as I was. He made me feel at home whenever I was with him. He would wrap me in his strong arms and draw me close. We fit well together.

Finally, I belonged. And I was safe.

I instantly liked Brad's mom. Miss Ruth was just as rough and crass as Brad, but had a secretly tender heart. She smoked constantly and only used her false "choppers" on special occasions. Most of the time, they sat in a jar beside the kitchen sink. Ruth didn't mince words and often spoke out of the side of her mouth.

I not only liked Miss Ruth, I loved her.

I didn't get to meet Brad's dad. Don had battled leukemia for ten years before his body had had enough.

Brad had watched his dad, a strong tower of a man, become beaten down with disease and medicine. Don was not a spiritual man but a man of few words and strong morals. He died just before Brad and I met.

It would take decades for Brad or me to fully recognize the impact of losing that father role.

He watched them both, each looking for more than the other could provide. It wasn't wrong to find a "together fit," but their reasons were wrong.

"Children, you look for Me in the ones you love. You will find a trace and cling to hope that it will lead to more—to Me.

"Instead, you will stumble and fall. You are ill-equipped without Me.

"Each of you will resent that the other is unable to fulfill you, so you both will strive and become parched. You don't see that it is I you desire.

"I alone can provide what you are longing for."

Brad smoked on occasion, and I didn't care for that. Then, when he told me that tobacco wasn't the only thing he smoked, I was more than disappointed.

Pot was a deal breaker for me. It didn't matter how much I liked the guy. I didn't want to be part of that lifestyle. I'd given him intimacy, but he had kept this from me. It surprised and hurt me that I hadn't seen it before.

Smoking weed wasn't a big deal to Brad, and he didn't see why it was to me. But it was a line I wasn't willing to cross, and I wasn't interested in being bound up with someone who was willing to cross it for himself. As Christmas rolled around, we stopped seeing each other.

It was a huge letdown. I missed being with him. In the absence of Brad, I felt the isolation of my home life crowding in again. I'd lost my escape.

During this season I visited Dad and Miss Ellie on occasion, but they had a new life now with Christine. I really wanted to know this little sister, but I couldn't shake the feeling that I was the outsider.

I didn't recognize it at the time, but I applied the same reasoning Dad had used in keeping loosely connected with us. I didn't want to disturb the good family unit he had going on.

My high school friends had gone to college the year before, and I didn't have any other friends besides Brad. I was lonely. I didn't know what else to do, so after the holidays, I enrolled in a local community college.

I actually was relieved for my college classes to start. It gave me something to focus on despite my academic challenges. I signed up for a photography class knowing I would need something of interest to keep me motivated through the other classes.

Two weeks into it I dropped my English class so I could keep my head above water. I soon discovered, that while I lacked enthusiasm for book work, photography and the darkroom fascinated me. I loved spending time in creative ways that weren't measured by my challenged reading and retention skills.

A few weeks later, I was heading to my car from morning classes. I admired the sun filtering through the trees in the crispness of the cool February day. As my eyes followed the path, I noticed a young man standing facing me. The shadow of the branches hid his face.

It appeared as though he were facing me directly—purposely standing there. I didn't know what to do, so I continued walking forward, trying not to look uncomfortable. A few more steps and I could tell he was looking directly at me. I felt relieved that there were other students walking nearby.

What's with this guy, and why's he blocking my pathway?

Not knowing where else to go without appearing threatened, I reminded myself that it was daytime, so I needn't fear. I tried to look preoccupied with my books. Then I recognized him.

It was Brad. His arms were crossed and his feet were set in a stance of determination. "I miss you, and I think you miss me too," he said as I approached him.

What? Man, this guy is bold.

"I'm right, aren't I?" he said. It was more of a statement than a question. There was that confidence again. Where I lacked, he overcompensated. He added, "I think we should make this work."

I was a little stunned, having not spoken with him for weeks. He continued. "Admit it. You miss me too." It was abrupt but true.

He was asking me to agree to work it out without first addressing the issue. He didn't say he would turn away from pot. When I brought it up, he took my hand and said he cared more about spending time together. "And if it's that important to you, then I will."

Without recognizing it, doubt took root inside. I *wanted* to believe him, and I didn't want to be alone.

Acceptance, desire, and ease in being with Brad overshadowed the nagging doubt. It was there. I just didn't want to deal with it. I suspected he still favored the occasional lure of the high.

But Brad was *my* great escape, even more than running. Instead of going home from school or work, I had a place—a person—to go to. And he cared about Ben and Jenny.

"Hey, let's take your sister to the drive-in tonight," he said, and with that he'd reached a tender place in me.

I used Brad to fill the gaping hole within me. When I was with him, I escaped the crazy, nauseating roller coaster. I wanted someone to belong to, and I began to believe I had found that person in Brad. We appealed to each other's attraction and desires. Quickly, I found myself giving in to physical longings, going further than I'd wanted to before marriage.

Finally, I told Brad I had made a commitment to myself to not have sex until marriage. "That's cool. We can do other things" he said.

And we did. We went far enough that it was too close not to complete what we'd begun. We were back at the same compromising place. I reasoned that it wasn't fair to take him to the point of desire but not to complete it, so I gave in.

One evening Brad suggested we talk about it. "We need to talk. It's not easy to say this, but we need to discuss it."

My heart rose. *He wants me to wait and honor my desire for purity.*

"You mean a lot to me, and I don't want us to be in a compromising situation we may both regret." As he spoke, I sat up, encouraged and relieved. He continued. "I care about you, about us, and what might happen."

I smiled, raising my eyebrows. "Okay. So . . . ?"

"So I made an appointment for you to get birth control." He smiled, taking my hands in his.

Wait. What? I was confused. I was glad he couldn't read my thoughts. Quickly, I gave a knowing reply. "Oh, yeah. You're right."

He squeezed my hands, shaking them gently. I sensed a weakness, a question in his eyes. He quickly pressed on. "I'll go with you if you want."

Now I was embarrassed—embarrassed to have hoped he would partner with me to help honor my morals and embarrassed that I was being told I needed to take precaution so I wouldn't get pregnant. I was disappointed. Even deeper was the embarrassment to myself that I had compromised my standards—my purity.

I went by myself to get birth control. And a piece of me died. Innocence had already been long gone. Now purity was gone as well. Worse, I'd given it away myself. In its place a heavy, dark shadow of shame took up occupancy.

The heavenly Father grieved. Her thoughts were void of Him though He remained as close as He'd always been. She was no longer a child but a young woman equipped with a strong, healthy body complete with God-given qualities and desires. He'd also provided her with a sound mind.

As He shook his head in dismay, a mane of pearl-white locks danced upon His massive shoulders. "Child, still I wait for you."

Brad and I spent all our spare time together. For his birthday I dressed up as a cowgirl with a sheriff's badge after secretly arranging with his manager for an extended weekend off. I had planned a road trip to the Mexican gulf. I liked adventure, and I was glad to have someone to share it with.

The following Christmas, Brad gave me string of real pearls. It was an extravagant gift. I knew he'd worked hard to save for it. I began to consider that he was serious about our relationship.

One night Brad came over for dinner; Nick was cooking. Our appetites were piqued as the aroma of fresh-baked lasagna filled the kitchen while we waited. We started rattling off our favorite foods. I mentioned a few of Grandma P's specialties: "Chicken cacciatore and sponge cake with real whipped topping and fresh strawberries."

Mom chimed in. "Brad, she's an escargot girl!"

It was true. Each year, she and Nick had taken me to a high-end restaurant for my birthday.

"If you're serious about this girl," Mom teased, "you need to know she likes the good stuff."

A few months later, Brad asked me to dress up for a special dinner date. "I have a surprise." He told me.

Brad had found a restaurant that served escargot. The dinner was amazing but Brad was acting odd. He was unusually serious and awkward—very unlike himself. I was uncomfortable.

What's wrong with him?

After dinner he took me to a private room, where he had wine and cheese waiting. I didn't have a clue. I just knew I was stuffed and didn't want to hurt his feelings. I was trying to figure out why he was so obsessed with all the food.

And why's he acting so weird?

Then he knelt on the floor and pulled a ring from his pocket.

What?!

He was serious.

Does he know that marriage is forever?

He said the words. "Shelly, will you marry me?"

I was in shock. How had I not seen this? *Does he know that once I say yes—it means we're going to spend the rest of our lives together?*

I not-so-romantically asked, "Are you sure you want to do this?"

We are too young. He's twenty-two, and I am only eighteen.

I could see in his eyes, he meant it. I think I saw more than I wanted to acknowledge of our immaturity and ignorance. I still had deep-rooted doubt. I also saw that he was sincere. To the best of his ability, he wanted to spend his life with me.

"Yes!" I nodded and smiled with tears. "Yes of course! Yes."

I couldn't wait to tell Ben and Jenny. I knew they liked Brad.

I wonder what Mom, Dad, and Nick will think.

I loved to hold the ring up to the sun to watch it sparkle. It amazed me that someone would want to marry *me*. Someone would give me a diamond ring because he wanted *me* to be *his*.

Other than getting married, we never really talked about dreams and plans. We were content just to be together.

As with so many other things, I had given up aspirations of pursuing the modeling career. I lacked confidence. Even so, I longed to see the rest of the world, and college only made my head spin. So, instead of signing up for another semester of college, I saved up and enrolled in a travel school so I could become a travel agent. I would fulfill my dreams by going to faraway places and meeting people of other cultures. The school was more technical than I'd hoped, but I would make it through.

A year and a half later, Brad and I married. Jenny was my brides-maid, and Christine was my flower girl. Miss Ellie didn't make it to the wedding, but she had sewn Christine's dress. I didn't recognize the time she'd put into it until years later. It had been her way of contributing her special gift. Dad and Nick both walked me down the aisle. It appeared we were one big happy family.

Soon after the wedding, I graduated from travel school and found a job at Quality Inn International. It wasn't the dream I'd gone to school for, but it was the travel industry.

Brad and I secured a little apartment that we furnished ourselves. I was Mrs. Busby.

The Son of God smoothed His mighty hand along a seamless cloth of white linen spread over an enormous table. It was one of many such tables in the Great Banquet Hall. He weaved among the tables, His magnificent robe, trailing behind, rustling like the sound of leaves in the fall.

The Wise King snatched a glance downward, looking on the earthly scene below.

"Marriage. My sacred union, a holy covenant, man and woman becoming one, the foundation to family."

He appeared to savor the word—family. His voice boomed from His mighty chest and the word sprang again from His lips in an explosion of sound and color that shot across the great hall and echoed like many drums.

He looked at the Father and smiled sadly, placing two more rough stones on the linen. "They are ignorant and naive. They will continue on their broken path, and they will hurt each another."

The Father nodded, touching the stones engraved with their names. The King squeezed His Father's shoulder with great affection as He passed.

"The Holy Spirit will teach them to love."

Brad and I didn't have friends in common, but we spent time with family and were happy being together.

Brad continued his last semester of tech school. About that time, his brother moved to Southern California. Greg had a great job in the fast-growing electronics industry. He felt confident that he could get Brad a professional job with his company once Brad graduated.

I'd always loved visiting California, but the thought of moving to SoCal scared me. It was such a big move, and I would be far from Ben and Jenny. Plus, the thought of living in the "beautiful people place" intimidated me. I was insecure enough as it was. How would I compete for Brad's affections when he would be surrounded by the temptation of beautiful beach girls?

I was sure I wasn't enough. I couldn't compare. That was reason enough for me *not* to go. Brad argued that the good jobs were in California. The choice was made, but not the way I expected.

Our first summer married, Brad and his sister's husband, Jim, got into a rift about something. In anger Jim shared with me that Brad was still smoking weed. He had been all along.

Brad denied it at first but eventually chose not to fight it. He defended himself by saying, "How can you be so opposed when you haven't even tried it? You don't really know unless you give it a go."

We went round and round until I gave in again. I tried it. In fact, I smoked several times over a week and a half. I *tried* to like it. I wanted to be on the same page with my husband. My experience only confirmed that I *didn't* like it. In fact, I hated it more than before I tried it.

I understood wanting to escape to process and clear one's mind. Running served as an escape for me. It's where I could process my thoughts.

To me weed was an escape; but you went nowhere except to a cloudy haze of apathy. I didn't want any part of it. Brad thought I valued my ideals over him; I thought he valued his choices over me.

At that time Greg's offer of a job came through. Sunny Southern California offered sandy beaches, beautiful sunset skies, and opportunity in large system computers. Who wouldn't go?

Brad went without me. He told me I was welcome to join him, but he was going either way. It was clear that he would be living his life his way. I moved back in with Mom and Nick.

In the mornings I'd leave for work. In the evenings I'd come home and run, then go to Momma Ruth's, where I'd fall asleep, wake up, drive home again to sleep, then start over. It wasn't awkward spending so much time with Momma Ruth. In fact, she was the one person I felt most at ease and at home with. We were happy just to sit and read, do puzzles, or watch an old movie until we fell asleep. Then I'd wake up to go home.

Even so, it felt as if I was moving backward. I was twenty years old, and I didn't know how to start either legal separation or divorce. I knew Brad wasn't going to do anything one way or the other. He wouldn't file for a divorce. He would just do his own thing.

I could have revisited my dream of being a travel agent, but I lacked confidence. I was afraid to do it alone.

A strange thing happened then. Nick came to my rescue. He saw my struggle when my self-worth crashed, and came to me with a proposal. "Let's take a drive," he said. We got in the car and he drove us to the other side of town.

I didn't know where he was going, and I didn't care. We ended up at a car dealership. "C'mon" Nick said, inviting me to get out of the car and walk the rows with him.

I thought he was running an errand. Maybe one of the guys from the carpool had left his wallet in Nick's van. Instead, Nick began looking at sports cars.

"What are you doing?" I asked. I knew he and Mom weren't in the market for a new car. He stopped at a sporty little gold Fiero 2M4, looked at me, and smiled. "Just for fun," he said.

He found a salesman and had me test-drive the car. It was shiny, pretty, fun, and fast. *Oh my gosh! I'm having fun!* I considered Nick's act of kindness. The only car I'd driven was my rusty, old, dying Honda. I pushed the knobs and buttons. It had a music system and a sun roof. Nick was having as much fun as me.

He then asked to speak with the salesman. In a short time he had managed to negotiate an incredible deal. I was shocked that I could afford the payments. Nick was elated to cosign, knowing I would be good to make payments.

I would never suggest buying a car to heal a wounded ego, but

Nick had great intentions, and it really boosted me through a rough time.

Eventually I went to visit Brad with the hope of figuring out what we were going to do. We'd have to discuss next steps sooner or later.

He picked me up from LAX airport and took me to Redondo Beach. I was captivated by the rushing waves on the shoreline. There were plenty of beach beauties, but I was relieved to find just as many normal people. Brad really seemed happy for me to be there. After all, we were still married and very young and immature.

I had booked a room for myself at a hotel nearby. I didn't want to stay at Greg's, where Brad was living. I knew they would be smoking.

We had a great weekend, spending time at the beach. I wanted our marriage to work. Driving to the airport, Brad spoke honestly. He didn't believe smoking weed was wrong. He walked me to the airplane terminal. "Take as much time as you need, but think about it, Shelly. Do you love me enough to accept me as I am?"

I didn't know what to do. It appeared that I was the deciding factor in whether or not the marriage would work.

But hadn't *he* left with or without me? Didn't he choose to continue smoking despite my convictions?

He who keeps the annals of time, watching over kings and lords, orphans and paupers, cast His eyes upon His wayward daughter.

"He is your husband. You are one now, child.

"I will teach you to love. And I will show him My ways.

"But daughter, you must turn to Me first. You can only understand love when you know Me."

I returned to Phoenix knowing no one else could make the choice for me. Mom and Nick had welcomed me back home, but I couldn't stay long. I was an adult and couldn't go back.

In the end I opted for an interview with Lincoln Savings and Loan in Irvine, California. They hired me and offered me a position the following week.

The Shepherd-King watched the two, needy and compromising, selfish and arrogant.

He looked past who they were and saw who He created them to be.

"They have much to learn about themselves and one another—a lump of clay, water and flour. They will remain a formless lump until they receive the oil of My presence, providing pliability to be shaped."

His eyes scanned over His banquet tables, adorned with both simple, rough stones and luminescent jewels. He glanced back at the young couple. "Yes, I will fashion this lump. They will become My vessel, precious stones reflecting My light."

7

THE GIFT

*E*ach weekend I scoured the newspaper ads and drove through the beach communities, looking for a place Brad and I could afford.

Before long we found a tiny apartment one block from the beach. We loved the small community, and I lived for my beachside runs.

Family often came to visit us in Southern California. "Hey, Shell," we would often hear, "mind if we come to visit? We could use some time on the beach." Mom and Nick came. Ben and John came. Jenny flew in several times. There was so much to see, but we always ended up spending most of the time sinking our feet into the sand while hanging out at the beach.

If we didn't have guests, we were exploring one beach community or another. When I was off work and Brad was working, I would find a new beach trail to run. I couldn't get enough of the briny air and constant coastal breeze. The beach life became our life. Eventually we made our way to Huntington Beach.

Though nothing really changed in our relationship, Brad and I settled into our norm. We managed through our differences.

The Master had fashioned a blueprint for the young couple's unique assignment. It was secured in the treasury of hope, tagged for a designated time.

The Holy Spirit shadowed the young couple everywhere they went. The veil that kept Him invisible was thick, like the grace He shielded them with.

At the appointed time the Holy Spirit breathed hope on the couple and whispered, "I bring you the King's gift."

The Master was pleased with His plan. "Yes, a gift will do them good."

Huntington Beach, Surf City, USA, spring 1989.

The morning mist began to lift as the sun cast rays through the marine haze. The air was salty, and the gentle breeze beckoned me as I stepped out the door.

It was still too cold to surf, though I would have liked to. I wasn't much of a surfer, but the rush of riding a wave took my breath away. I closed my eyes and pictured a wave beneath my legs. I'd have to wait for a warmer day.

I would never tire of this place. In the summer Brad and I walked the beach to the pier. The closer we came to the pier, the thicker the stream of tourists flooded the streets and boardwalk.

As we neared the crowds, we'd exchange glances and smile. We each knew the other was thinking the same thing: *We live here.*

After three years this was our home, and for all my former fears, I had to admit I loved it.

But on this particular morning, I had other things on my mind. I couldn't get down to the beach fast enough. I had to feel the cold water, the sinking sand and pounding waves. I ached for the tide to come in and wash the fogginess from my head. I needed to get my thoughts straight. Flip-flops off, toes scrunching, I reached the sand. The air was cool, but the sun on the sand was warm.

Think. THINK.

When did this happen?

I watched the waves cap over, but all I could think about was that one tiny little line crossing the other. It was *positive*, not negative.

POSITIVE.

Really? Pregnant. Me?

We had agreed we weren't going to have children. We had only just begun to settle into a mutual acceptance of each other's differences. There were so many things we wanted to do. We were selfish, and we knew it and were okay with it. It was *our* lives, right?

Only recently had we entertained the *remote* possibility that *one* day, we might actually consider having a child. Maybe. Certainly, it wouldn't be for a good eight to ten years.

How am I going to tell Brad? What will he say?

What would he think? This was his life too. Maybe the test stick was faulty. I'd get another. But deep down, I knew. I also knew that this was *life*. LIFE! And I could not, would not, stop it.

Our lives were about to be forever changed. Like the riptide that catches you when you don't think you're far out, the course of our lives would suddenly and drastically change forever.

I would tell Brad when he got home. It was Saturday, and he had been called in to work, but first I would take another test to be sure.

I burrowed my feet in the soft sand. It was late March, and the chilly breeze refreshed me. What would our lives look like now?

This was so not the plan.

I grabbed a fistful of sand and clenched it tightly. Ever so slightly I loosened my grip. Countless grains eased out. In a moment my hand was empty.

Later, Brad looked at me, baffled and speechless. There had been one night . . . Valentine's Day. We'd gone out with Greg and friends from the job site, and out of our norm, we drank. We were both too frisky to be careful. We thought we'd caught ourselves in time.

The second and third tests were positive. It took a couple of days walking around stunned before it really sank in.

We agreed to take the week to decide if we would have a *baby*. But deep inside, I knew there was no option. There was new life *in me*. We hadn't planned for it, but it was there. It was perfectly natural and still it seemed . . . miraculous.

Me. Pregnant.

It was a long week not talking about it. In fact, we didn't talk much at all, consumed with inner questions.

What would our lives look like with a child?

What if he doesn't want it?

My vision of our future had already shifted to include the child that was forming inside me, and that scared me too. We were so ill-equipped.

Each day my identity was shaping into something new. I was becoming someone's mother. *We* were no longer just Brad and me. This was not a choice for me. I had compromised enough. I knew this child had a place in the world. Brad would have to want the same thing on his own.

Finally, the decision day came. It was a relief just to be talking. It had been awkward not talking about it all week. We voiced the questions we'd been contemplating.

"How will a baby affect our future?"

"How will we raise it?"

"Could we give away our own baby?"

The answer to that question was easy. We couldn't. And if we couldn't give away our own baby, we certainly couldn't deprive this child of life.

"How can we afford a baby?"

We couldn't, not with the plans we had. Those plans would have to be shelved until . . . ? This was a *life* that we had formed together.

Strangely, unexpectedly, this new twist of fate was inviting. Once we gave ourselves permission to let go of our plans, new excitement arose in us. *We* were going to have a *baby*. It was new territory, and new thoughts and contemplations rushed in like the afternoon tide. The focus of our lives was no longer Brad or me, but the building of a *family*.

The ocean breeze picked up and swept over them with a sudden gust that caught them off guard. The young couple looked to the sky, expecting to see rain clouds forming, but found only the bright sun.

The Shepherd passed before them, having sifted through their thoughts and new dreams. His eyes shone bright seeing the child within. The life growing within the young woman was truly a gift—to her, to the couple, and even to the Kingdom.

"Life. My ever-increasing kingdom—my perfect plans!"

Warmer months came. The child growing inside was a boy; I was sure of it. Dr. Rosales scheduled a sonogram and it was confirmed; we were having a son.

That night I poured myself into bed next to Brad. *There it is again.* I'd eaten more grapes. *Maybe it's the grapes.*

"Brad! It did it again!"

"Huh? What did what?"

I put my hands on my belly, expecting to feel something but didn't. "The earthquake thingy. It happened this afternoon. Oh, I think it's him! Or grapes."

Half-asleep, Brad mumbled, "What? Earthquake? Grapes? Okay, that's nice. G' night, Shell."

I lay still, willing it to happen once more.

Is that you, little person inside?

He smiled. Among a myriad of night whispers came a favorite sound—the faint beating of a little boy's heart, growing in sync with the Creator.

Only six weeks to go. The baby kicked my ribs as I lay in bed, thinking about the weekend. I could barely roll to the other side to sit up.

We've got to get rid of this waterbed.

Today was my day to fly to Phoenix. The sun flooded the bathroom through the little window box. I looked in the mirror.

Ugh.

I grimaced at my reflection. My face looked like a puffy doughnut. I wished I could just unzip the pregnancy suit even for a day to feel my original body. I'd never been big and hated feeling sluggish with extra weight.

I can't wait to run—without an attached bowling ball.

I'd take a walk to the beach before packing for the long, weekend trip. The waves would feel good rushing over my feet. My entire body seemed to be sore all the time now. I put on a cotton dress. It was roomy and hid the extra curves.

Looking at my roundness, I spoke to my baby belly. "Jake, I love you little one, but it really stinks trying to get around like a giant walking water balloon."

The flight from LAX to Phoenix was short and uneventful. I was looking forwarding to seeing family. Mom and Aunt Laurie were throwing me a baby shower.

Mom and Dad's childhood friend, Aunt Laurie, had flown in from St. Louis. Jenny drove up from college. Miss Toni and Joanna would be there. Ben promised to come even though showers were a girl-thing.

Back home with family, hanging out at the pool, we caught up and reminisced about old times. Aunt Laurie mentioned hoping to visit

Dad before she flew back. "Your Dad and I were friends before I met your mom in high school, you know."

I knew. I'd sifted through Mom's old pictures dozens of times over the years. I loved hearing the stories about life "back in the day." Dad and Aunt Laurie had been friends since kindergarten.

I was looking forward to seeing Dad, Miss Ellie, and Christine and couldn't wait to see Dad's face when he saw my big belly, round with baby.

I'd missed Dad's call earlier, so I called him back. "Hey Dad, so when do I get to see you? Mom and Aunt Laurie are throwing me a baby shower." Aunt Laurie was sitting near me on the other couch, reading.

I added, "I want to see you. I can't wait for you to see how round I am. He's been kicking all day, and I want you to feel him, Dad."

We small-talked a few minutes before I said, "So, when can we get together? The shower is tomorrow at one o'clock, and Aunt Laurie goes back Sunday morning. She'd really like to see you before she goes." Aunt Laurie looked up and smiled.

The line was silent. It was always awkward scheduling visits. Maybe he didn't understand. I added, "We'd love to maybe have dinner with you and Miss Ellie and Christine, but I don't want Ellie to have to make anything."

Aunt Laurie whispered, "Tell him I want to treat!"

Nick walked in, dirty and covered in grease from working on the van. He wiped the sweat dripping off his face. You could smell the sweaty grease across the room. Quietly, he washed at the kitchen sink.

"Maybe we can go out for pizza," I continued trying to entice Dad. "Aunt Laurie wants to treat."

Dad wasn't responding. I racked my brains.

Did I leave someone out? No.

Had I presumed upon anyone? No. Shoot! What am I missing?!

Dad lived a half mile away, but it felt as if he were there in the room. I could see him pacing, shoulders rolled slightly forward but relaxed, one hand in his pocket. His brows would be knitted in contemplation. He, too, was trying not to hurt anyone.

Who was he protecting? What was he protecting anyone from?

I didn't understand.

I dared to ask, "Is there a problem?" A lump rose in my throat. Laurie looked up again as Nick lingered at the sink.

He finally spoke.

"Well, kiddo, ya see . . ."

Something was wrong.

No!

I knew where this was going.

No!

I looked at my swollen ankles, suddenly wishing I were alone, in a private conversation. Shame came out of nowhere like the morning mist back home at the beach.

This was supposed to be a celebration weekend, a time for family to say things like: "Woo-HOO! Baby is almost here." "You go, little momma; we're so excited for you." And "You CAN do this. We're here for you!"

My abdomen balled up, tensing like a rock. Braxton-Hicks.

Great.

They came at least once each day.

I held the phone away from my mouth, sucking a big gulp of air. With my free hand I pressed my stomach, trying to counter the muscles. It was tight. Quietly, I blew away from the phone. *Okay, little guy; not too much longer.*

Dad explained that he'd really like to see me, but he didn't want to put Ellie in a bad place, and, well, if Laurie was there, "that just wouldn't be right."

I took another deep breath. "Okay. Well, do you want to meet somewhere for pizza with just Aunt Laurie and me?"

Of course he wants to see me, right?

I closed my eyes, picturing Dad as he paced.

His next words sucked the wind out of me. "Well, if you don't accept me with my wife, then you have no business with me."

Eyes wide-open, I gasped for air.

Did I hear him right?

Maybe Dad had had a bad day; maybe tensions were high at the plant.

Was it the baby shower? I knew Miss Ellie wouldn't want to be there; it would have been awkward for her.

Didn't he know by now how much I longed to be part of his and Miss Ellie's life?

And, damn, I wish there were a longer cord on this phone.

"Breathe, child. Just breathe."

And whose voice was that, anyway?

I heaved in air, blood rising and heart sinking, reaching for words —any words.

"Okay, Dad. Ummm . . . I don't understand. I don't know what to say. I want to see you. Aunt Laurie was looking forward to seeing you too. I . . . I don't understand."

Click. Dial tone. No goodbye.

"Breathe."

I looked at the phone in my hand; my hands were sweating.

No. That didn't just happen, did it?

Brad, I wish you were here!

Aunt Laurie looked puzzled.

Did she hear what he just said?

I couldn't crumble now. I turned to anger instead, letting it cover and protect me like a quick scab over a gaping wound. Like a scab, anger is ugly, buffering and masking the wound beneath.

I grabbed the side of the couch for leverage with my bloated center of gravity and slowly stood. Anger rose with me.

Nick had lingered in the kitchen, surveying the situation. I looked at Aunt Laurie, and with an apologetic tone in my voice said, "Umm, Dad's not going to be able to get together."

She'd heard and offered to call him back. I attempted a meager smile. "I don't think that'd help."

I picked up the phone again and dialed. Adrenaline kicked in and my anger elevated.

"Hello." Dad answered.

"Dad. I'm coming over now. I want you to see me as I am."

"Okay." He must have had a few too many drinks or something. "You can come over, but like I said, you need to come alone. Don't bring anyone with you."

Floored, I could feel my heart racing. Nick was unusually quiet, still busying himself in the kitchen. Mom came into the living room, arms full of shower decorations. "What's going on?"

"I'm going over to Dad's."

I wanted him to *see me*. I wanted him to see me pregnant. I was tired of feeling invisible. I wasn't a complication. I was his daughter—pregnant with his first grandchild.

I was furious. I needed him.

He can't take this away, too.

Confused, Mom repeated, "Will somebody tell me what's going on?" Laurie pulled her into the formal living room and told her what had happened.

Calmly, coming out from the kitchen galley, Nick offered, "Shelly, you want me to go over and talk to him?"

I stared at him numbly. At least my stomach had loosened back to normal.

He added, "I will. Your dad and I know each other. Sometimes men just need to talk."

I knew he would—in a peaceful, diplomatic way. They worked at the same nuclear plant and saw each other often. They'd maintained a cool but civil relationship. Even with all of Nick's crazy episodes, he'd never lost it with regards to Dad.

Even with all the junk we'd gone through, Nick had never spoken ill of Dad. He had watched my relationship with Dad deteriorate over the years. When Dad had missed events or was emotionally detached and unavailable to Ben, Jenny, or me, Nick had always offered a plausible excuse, reassuring us that our dad loved us.

"No. Thanks. I need to do this myself." I went to my old room to put on a fresh shirt. I was sweaty again.

I waddled back into the living room and found Mom's keys. "Mom, I need to borrow your car."

Dad lived only six blocks north of us. The drive was too short. I didn't have a plan yet.

What am I going to say?

It was evening now, and the porch lamp lighted the walkway.

It was always bittersweet coming to Dad's house. The house had the exact same floor plan as our home before the divorce. That had been my home—a happy one—the home we brought Jenny home to initially. I loved that Dad's home was like our old one, but here now I was just an occasional visitor. I had visited in my darkest hours but was not welcome to *live* here. I hated that.

I could feel my heart pounding as I approached the door. I took a breath and knocked.

Dad opened the door. "Hey kiddo. I didn't know if you'd actually come or not."

"Hi, Dad."

"Why don't ya come on in?"

"Dad, you said some pretty hurtful things. You *hung up* on me. I can't come in there with Miss Ellie and have you talking like I've done something against her. I wanted us all to be together. Laurie wanted to meet with you too. All of you."

"Well, you just don't understand what it's like for Ellie, now, do you?"

No. I didn't. I had always longed to understand. I really liked Miss Ellie. I knew she worked hard to welcome us kids. It didn't help that Ben and I looked so much like Mom.

As kids, we'd enjoyed Sunday evening dinners at Dad's, helping prepare the meals and washing dishes afterward with Miss Ellie. Dad had no idea how I'd craved for us kids to be accepted as part of his new family.

Miss Ellie was a good woman. I saw how she loved Dad. She also had to share him with us. It was just awkward.

And now there was an awkward, silent pause. In that moment I wondered . . . Had Dad tried too hard to protect his new family from his old, broken one? Had he inadvertently placed himself as a wedge between us all?

"Are you going to come into my home or not?"

My home.

The words stung.

"Okay, Dad. You don't get it, do you? I'm trying to tell you. I'm not part of the past. I'm here now. I'm gonna have this baby pretty soon. This is my *life*, Dad. I want you to share in it, but you just won't let that happen." I was trembling now.

Dad went into a fury, ranting as he pushed his way out the door. This was so uncharacteristic for Dad. He advanced, cussing, thrusting his finger at me with his words.

I retreated down the walkway.

Oh, God. This isn't happening. I can take it from Nick, but this is Dad.

"Well, if you ever want to be part of my life, then you just better get your crap together and keep that bitch of a mother the hell out of my life. And screw you, and I don't care what you do with your life."

I knew he couldn't mean it, but he didn't stop the words or the advancing.

In shock, I backed away toward the car. He started to push at me. That was enough. Red-hot anger soared through me.

"Don't. You. Dare! I'm pregnant, Dad! Do you *see me*?" I stood up tall and determined, not backing up any farther. "*You* get away from *me*." These were hardest words I never wanted to say.

Who was he so angry at? Who was he really addressing? Did he see someone else in his mind's eye? His last words cut deeply: "You just get the hell off my property. GO! Get out of here!" He stormed back into the house.

Shaking, I fumbled to get in the car.

The short drive back to Mom's house was surreal. I claimed pregnancy tiredness and sequestered myself into my old room. The room was too familiar. It appeared warm and bright, but in truth, it was a place of loneliness and rejection.

I replayed the scene over and over in my head.

God? Where are You?

What's wrong with me?

The little one kicked inside me, reminding me I was not alone.

I went about the remainder of the weekend as planned, numb from the sting of that night. I didn't discuss it with anyone.

On Sunday evening I flew back to LA. As the plane circled back for its final descent, the pitch-black expanse of ocean met the tiny lights of the big city. The plane lowered, weaving up and down ever so slightly. I always loved this part. It felt as if we sped up when we were actually slowing down.

I hadn't told Brad about the run-in with Dad. The scene replayed in my head for the umpteenth time. Bluish-green runway lights appeared to grow as we descended. We were close. I looked at my watch, calculating the minutes until I'd find myself safely back in Brad's arms. Maybe I wouldn't even tell him.

Brad picked me up in the Jeep. Most of the time we had the top off.

The wind felt great, but it was hard to hold a conversation. Usually, we just pumped up the tunes.

The 405 Freeway moved quick Sunday evenings, probably the only time that it did. I drank in the cool, salty air and appreciated not having to talk.

Exiting the freeway, Brad broke the silence, shouting through the wind. "Mind if we get some tacos? Not much to eat at home. Worked all weekend."

Food didn't sound good. There'd been plenty to eat at Mom's, but I hadn't had an appetite since the night with Dad. Still, I said, "Sounds great." Brad would need to eat.

Breaking my taco shell in little pieces, I told Brad about the weekend, glossing over the events with Dad.

Brad was really hungry.

I bet he didn't eat all weekend.

No need to weigh him down with more family junk. He'd get angry with Dad, and then it would only get messier. Besides, Brad looked good. The sight of him put me at ease.

Later, as we lay in bed, Brad cradled me, one hand on my belly, the other tucking me close. *This is home.*

"Hey." I turned so I could see his eyes.

He kissed my forehead. "Yeah?"

"It's really good to be home."

He squeezed me closer.

Before long his breathing slowed, and I knew he was asleep. Safe in his arms, I finally let my tears loose. Dad's words had cut deep. I hoped he'd call to retrieve his words, but I was sure he wouldn't.

I knew deep down Dad loved me.

But how did this . . .

Why . . .

Tears fell silently on my pillow as exhaustion drew me to sleep. Faintly, I heard a dreamlike voice . . .

"Breathe, child. Breathe."

A thick mist rolled off the sea to the nearby shore as the Holy Spirit quietly invaded the little bedroom, delivering sleep and dispensing truth with hope.

"Yes, he knows you love him. He loves you.

"I hold his heart, and I know what has sifted through it. Like you, he has been crushed and broken.

"He has his own battles and his own story that will break your heart. But you are far from the place of understanding.

"Breathe hope, child, and follow Me. I make all things new. Watch and see."

It was late fall, with clear blue skies and a balmy breeze coming off the ocean. The summer tourists were gone, and the beaches were quiet again.

Nick had just moved to LA for temporary contract work with the union. He found an apartment eighteen miles inland. His work days were long, so we didn't see him often, limiting run-ins with his episodes. He expressed that he wanted us to call on him for help if we needed anything with the pregnancy.

He was such a strange mix of generosity and unpredictability.

I started maternity leave the week of Thanksgiving to get ready for Jake's arrival. He was due in two weeks. I smoothed my hand over my enormous belly. "We're close now, little guy."

Mom was due to fly in late the day before Thanksgiving. I was about to bake my first turkey. I had gone to the store several times, twice forgetting one ingredient, then another. I was just pleased that I'd gotten so far as to thaw the bird.

My belly tensed again. I'd had Braxton-Hicks contractions

throughout the pregnancy. Now they came several times a day. I was sore, numb, and achy. Brad was working the swing shift and wouldn't get off until midnight.

Nick called. "Hey, why don't I stop by and help ya get started with the turkey and stuffing." He was in a good mood. "I have a couple hours before I go pick up your mom." Nick was as eager as Mom to meet this little Jake. I could hear the excitement in his voice.

I could barely keep my eyes open. I wasn't feeling well, and the thought of sticking my hands in a raw turkey butt made me want to vomit. "Do you think we could just get started tomorrow morning instead of doing the prep tonight?"

"Sure, hon, but I have something I want to bring you. I think it'll do you good."

An hour later, Nick knocked on the door, bearing a pot of some strange vegetable soup I'd never heard of. He came in and warmed it up on the stove. "This is a special recipe. Have a bowl; then get some rest."

I wanted to get the pies baked, but it hurt to stand now, and the soup smelled delicious. I ate the soup and promised to take a nap.

"I'll pick up your mom later, and we'll be here in the morning." He headed for the door. "We can work on the meal together in the morning."

I don't know what he put in that soup, but I figured it was one of Grandma P's recipes. It was amazing and it filled me. There was so much I wanted to do, and it was still light out. I lay down . . .

Just twenty minutes or so.

The next thing I knew, I woke up and it was dark. I felt strange. I looked at the clock.

Five hours?!

And why did I feel so gross?

What?! I wet my pants! Ugh!

Then I felt more warmth wetting my sweatpants. I was up, heading for the bathroom.

Great. Now I can't even control my bladder.

Then another gush.

Oh!!! This is it! This is baby.

I cleaned up and put on fresh clothes. I could barely dial the phone. Brad answered, "Hey, how ya—"

I cut in, "It's time, Brad. It's time! I'm gonna go to the hospital."

There was a pause as he processed what I was saying. "What? Wait. Now?! Are you sure? How do you know?"

I explained the water breaking.

Brad assured me, "You're not driving yourself. I'm leaving now. Just wait. I'll be there as fast as I can." I could hear the excitement in his voice. It was after eleven o'clock the night before Thanksgiving. There wouldn't be much traffic, but coming from downtown LA to Huntington, he would have a good forty-five- to fifty-minute drive *if* he sped.

I called Dr. Rosales. He warmly reassured me. "Ah, good. It's a little early, but not too much. Okay, I'll be at the hospital in an hour. Go ahead and get situated. I'll see you soon."

My fingers shook with excitement as I dialed Nick to see if they'd made it back to his place from the airport, but there was no answer. I left an excited message, then headed back to the bathroom . . . wet again.

Brad, I hope you make it soon.

I checked my overnight bag and heard someone coming up the concrete steps to our little apartment. It had only been five or ten minutes; it couldn't be Brad.

There was a knock; chills went up my back. Our apartment was sequestered away above garages, overlooking an alley. It wasn't easy to find unless you knew where to go.

Who could it be at this hour Thanksgiving eve?

I imagined the headlines. "Robber Delivers Baby—Gets More Than He Bargained For."

Wait. Robbers don't knock . . . do they?

I just wouldn't answer. Again with the wetness. *Seriously?!*

Then I recognized voices. "Shelly, it's us!" It was Mom and Nick.

I opened the door. "How'd you know to come?"

We only had landlines back then. I gave Nick an inquisitive look. He understood. "I know. I just had this feeling all day."

This was better than Christmas Eve, except for the wetness.

"Brad's on his way from downtown. Hey, what did you put in that soup?"

He smiled. "Just soup."

Soon we heard wheels peeling down the alley. A minute later Brad was taking stairs two at time.

Early Thanksgiving morning, Jake was born. The sound of his voice shocked me. He was here. We'd known all along we would eventually meet this gift, but hearing his cry, holding his little body, and seeing his eyes astonished both Brad and me. We had a baby!

Eternal and magnificent, like a thousand shining diamonds casting millions of brilliant reflections, the Creator's light and splendor shimmered new LIFE.

He gave the child his first breath, eliciting a first cry. First to last, He would be there for every breath, stringing each together with the hope of His glory.

Jenny caught a flight and was there just after Jake arrived. We celebrated, each taking turns holding our new bundle. Eventually Mom, Nick, and Jenny left to get breakfast.

There was one more call—the most important one. I picked up the phone three times and put it back on the receiver.

I wanted Dad to know, but I was still reeling from the pain of our last run-in.

What if he hangs up on me?

"Call him." I felt the words more than heard them.

The nurse finished checking Jake's vitals, then placed him back in my arms. The words repeated again in my head—

"Make the call. Make it now. You will never get this day back."

I dialed Dad's number.

Christine answered—it was a welcome sound. "Hello?" (We didn't have caller ID back then.)

"Hey, Chris. It's Shelly. Happy Thanksgiving. How are you?"

"Hi, Shelly. Happy Thanksgiving to you too. I'm doing good. How are you?"

There was only kindness in her voice. That was all we had directly between us.

"I'm good. I'm calling to share some good news. Jake is here. He was born this morning. I'd like to tell Dad myself. Is he there?"

"Wow! That's great. Yeah. Hold on just a sec."

I began to sweat. *Is he still mad? Will he hang up?*

"Hello?"

"Hi, Dad."

"Well, hello. How are ya?"

It's awkward for him too.

I could hear the caution in his voice, but more than that, there was warmth in his tone. Five words. It's amazing how much you can tell from the tone of five little words when you know someone so well.

Sigh and a breath. "I'm good. I'm calling because, Dad, I wanted you to know that Jake was born this morning, just a little over an hour ago."

"Really? Well, I'll be."

If I closed my eyes I could see his labored smile. He'd been hurt too.

"I thought you'd would want to know," I said.

"Of course I do. This is a really important day. You sound good."

Swaddling the child with the grace of His presence, the Lord dispensed plans and assignments, gifts and callings. The child would grow to provoke others to the King's bidding, but first he would be used to reflect the King's Light, awakening his parent's hearts.

Our little family had grown. To look at us, it would appear we had the world in our hands. We were young, healthy, and had a beautiful baby boy.

Just after Jake was born, Brad gave me a gift I loved even more than the pearls. He bought Jake and me a Baby Jogger. It was a running partner and babysitter all in one. I could continue running while getting Jake out of the apartment for fresh air and sunshine. It was the perfect gift! We could run anytime, and we did.

Those days were full and rich, as we enjoyed the life-changing gift of a child. I would happily have stayed in this season for years, but weeks and months passed. We continued our daily beach runs, but soon Jake was using his own legs to get around.

Brad and I laughed watching him grow from dependent baby to fireball toddler. It was amazing that we had a child.

"Hey, let's take the jogger down to the pier. Jake can balance on the timbers."

We did everything together as a family.

Almost as soon as Jake learned how to walk, he *ran*. The boy ran everywhere, chasing birds on the shore, chasing other kids. If there wasn't someone or something to race or chase, Jake would find his own race.

We'd be playing at the beach and I'd hear his squeals. "Raaaaa!" He'd run, chasing the foamy water to meet the end of the wave at dry sand.

One day, after his usual run-and-chase, he tiptoed his way over the toasty sand to our spot by lifeguard stand 20. "Hot, Momma!"

"Yeah, honey, the sand is hot! You hungry, little man?" I asked. His fair skin was beginning to pink up despite the sunscreen. It was time to head home. He grunted in the affirmative.

"Okay, buddy," I said, "let's go home and get some real food. Get your Spidey-Mans on." Proudly, quickly, he sat down with his Spider-Man flip-flops and wrestled his boxy feet into them. This was his newly mastered big-boy task.

Arms filled with beach gear, we shuffled through the sand. Little legs took a while to climb the steps leading from the beach toward home. The boom of crashing waves gave way to the sound of cars passing on the Pacific Coast Highway.

More delightful than the sound of waves pouncing on the shore, I heard the slight *fffttt, fffttt, fffttt* of Jake's Spidey shoes scuffing along the pavement.

The ocean would always be here, but would I remember the sound of my little boy's flip-flops?

We made our way up the sandy street to the apartment. Brad would be home soon.

Who is that behind us?

I looked over my shoulder to the palms waving in the breeze. *Hmmm. No one.* I tightened my grasp on Jake's grainy little hand.

The rhythm of the waves and breeze resonated with His perfect cadence of

power and peace—a constant balanced force that the Protector would continuously offer the young mother in the trials to come.

The Father walked close behind mother and child, also taking note of the *fffttt, fffttt, fffttt* of the boy's sandals.

"Yes, daughter," He answered her unspoken question, "I will seal this sound in your heart. You won't forget."

To the towheaded boy, He spoke tender secrets, "You, son, are part of a much greater plan. I'm placing hope in your heart so that one day, you will carry the Light to those around you."

The Holy One continued to look on the children below for a moment, then fondly looked at His Son, and the twenty-four elders in His presence. He beamed with great pleasure seeing the children who'd made it home already.

The sight and sound were a combined orchestra of life as everyone tended to the tasks He'd appointed in preparation and anticipation of the coming Feast.

Even surrounded by the magnificent sea of people, the Father longed for more—for all—for those who'd not yet made it home.

The Son's eyes swept high and low, taking in the expanse of the great mansion and the movement of light and color within. The palace was more prestigious than any earthly dwelling, with grand rooms and open halls. Lush gardens and great stone fountains were dispersed throughout. Streams ran intermittently from within, flowing to its outer boundaries and the greater garden beyond.

Here in the King's great throne room, with sky-stretched ceilings and glassy sea, the bride would one day be presented to the Son before the court of the elders. His bride would be made up of all the children of God whose face and hearts are toward Him—from Adam and the great fathers of faith to those who will face earth's last days in its present state—and the King could hardly wait.

The Son looked to the Father and their eyes met. Their hopes were the same . . . that all would enter.

Outside the boundaries of the kingdom realm, the opposition pressed in on *the earthly battlefield. The Great War was won, but Death tenaciously pursued any who were unwilling to receive the King's invitation. The Dark One would prey upon the children of God to kill and destroy and devour with vehemence until the final hour. The wretchedness of evil clung close to the earth, thickening pervasively in a dark cloud among all the nations.*

Despite the dense fog of darkness, the sounds of the saints' prayers and songs of adoration continued to rise to the halls of heaven, piercing the darkness and loosening light and glory from above.

8

AT A CROSSROADS

om came to town frequently to see Nick and to visit us. At times Nick appeared to be doing much better. Unfortunately, after a day or two together, it was plain to see that he still suffered the same challenges. Eventually, his work project finished, and he returned to Phoenix.

Meanwhile, our little boy was growing up.

When Jake was three, we received an invitation to my cousin Robyn's wedding in St. Louis. Brad couldn't go because of work, but he bought a ticket for me. The rest of the family would be there, so it would be a great time for a family reunion.

I scheduled a visit with my cousin Marcy, Robyn's sister, before the wedding day. Our lives had changed so much now that we were moms.

We sat in her living room, laughing as we caught up. I was enjoying our late-afternoon conversation until Marcy brought up Nick.

"You know, Shelly, I love you and look forward to seeing you, but sometimes I wish Nick didn't come."

My stomach turned.

"What do you mean, Marcy?" I led her, hoping she was referring only to his occasional erratic behavior: "Like when he gets bent out of shape with a waiter?"

On several occasions we would be at a restaurant and Nick would find something wrong with his order. "Where's the manager?" he'd bluster. "You need to get him right now." Then he would make a big scene that would embarrass the whole party.

She laughed, knowing what I meant. Then she shifted in her chair and continued, a little more serious now. "No. I mean I really don't like to be alone with him. You know?"

I could feel the blood drain from my face. It was a strange sensation. I noticed I was holding my breath.

I took a long deep breath and paused. I didn't want to know more, but I had to. "Marcy, what are you talking about? When have you been alone with him?"

She went on to tell me how Nick had taken advantage of her sexually during different visits.

"Marcy, why didn't you tell anyone?" I was sickened and perplexed. He hadn't been sexual with me since I was thirteen. My mind started to wonder. If he had done that with Marcy, could he have done that with someone else too? "Marcy, do you know if he did anything to Robyn?"

The more I heard, the more I wanted to make her stop, but I had to know the truth. A wave of coldness took over me. I shuddered as I thought of the others affected.

I'm responsible. If I had pressed charges back then . . . And who else has there been? I could have prevented this.

Nick had not only turned to someone different, he had taken things much further.

My thoughts raced as I left Marcy's.

Was this the result of purposely forgetting and ignorantly moving on?

This couldn't continue. He had not been held accountable and had been handed no consequences. There was no reason for him to stop.

I felt robotic the next few days, interacting with the family. I tried to sort through the new information and get a clear perspective as the shock subsided. There were no private phones, so I couldn't discuss the situation with Brad. I would have to wait for an appropriate time and place to address the matter with Mom and Nick.

And how am I going to do that?

What I really wanted to do was catch the next flight back to California and never look back. A part of me was really sad too. I had seen Nick care for us over the years. I knew he loved us. I had grown to love him too. We were his family. But this was too much.

I didn't want anything to do with him. There was no point in trying to work it out. We'd already done that. Look where that got us.

I was also angry with Mom. I viewed her ignorance as cowardly and pathetic. She, too, like me, was indirectly responsible by enabling Nick to get away with his sickness. This was a crooked path, and I wanted off.

The Father was nonplussed by the unfolding scene. He wasn't surprised. Nothing was hidden from Him.

But His passion for the victim—His child—was white-hot. He looked down upon His brokenhearted daughter, so saddened by the sick truth she had just discovered, and yet so unaware of the One who could help her, if only she would call on Him.

"Wake up, child! Open your eyes to Me. You need Me."

Robyn's wedding took place at a beautiful art deco greenhouse known as the Jewel Box of Forest Park. It's bright and open, with more than four thousand panes of glass set in wrought iron. We were surrounded by the beauty of natural flora and plentiful sunshine. Even so, the world seemed to crowd in around me.

The dinner reception followed nearby at Culpepper's. The crowd was lively and the food was awesome. It was time for celebration, but I felt sick.

I couldn't look at Nick and didn't want to talk to Mom. We didn't know anyone but my aunt and cousins. I had to sit with family. I took the seat farthest from Nick. I tried to enjoy my dinner, but instead I pushed the food around my plate, unable to eat. Mom looked at my plate, "Are you okay?"

"Yes. Just not real hungry."

"Well, the food is really good; you should try the beef."

I tried to make conversation with Ben, but he was still irritated that twice now I'd made him sit next to Nick.

I wanted to get away. I got up and went to the ladies' room, then toured the restaurant. I didn't drink, so the bar wasn't an option.

Brad, I wish you were here.

Mom caught up with me my second time to the ladies' room. "Are you sure you're okay?"

I wanted to be left alone. "Yeah, Mom. I'm fine."

No! I'm not fine. Everything is NOT okay. It hasn't been for years. You would like it to be, so we could all just go dig our heads in the sand, like we did before.

This was not the place to talk about family matters.

The Most High God stood near with a full arsenal of new strength and unexpected, surpassing peace. He offered hope and healing, wisdom, righteousness, and justice.

He longed for his daughter to look up and see Him, to cry out for His help, though He knew she wouldn't.

She shut Him out, taking another drink of anger and indignation.

"Child, your anger will never achieve My righteousness or My justice."

Finally, the day came to an end. I couldn't wait to call Brad. I wouldn't have privacy to speak freely, but I longed to hear his and Jake's voices.

We had another day before we flew back to our respective homes. Aunt Vera announced she was treating everyone to a day at Six Flags. We had gone there together several times over the years. It had become somewhat of a tradition.

When, where, and how was I going to address this pressing issue? A day at the amusement park was not what I had in mind; it only delayed the inevitable. I would have to face Mom and Nick before we went our separate ways the next morning.

Fortunately, Marcy's husband, Joey, had been driving their car to manage transportation of our combined families. The guys drove with Joey, and the girls drove with Aunt Vera.

In the car, Mom started again with the questions. "Shelly, what is wrong?"

"Nothing, Mom."

"I can tell."

Aunt Vera, Marcy, Mom, Jenny, and I were all in the car together.

Okay, this is awkward.

"Nothing I want to talk about now."

At the park entrance we discussed where to go first. I suggested we split into two groups: those who would do the rides; and Mom, Nick, and Vera, who would go see the shows.

We agreed to meet midday for lunch. This gave me time to let Marcy know I would be telling Nick and Mom what I knew from what she had shared. I saw her hesitancy.

"Marcy, this can't go on," I urged. "He cannot do these things and get away with it. It's wrong."

She nodded, "I know. I shoulda said something sooner."

The two groups reconnected in the afternoon. I was no longer hiding my aversion to Nick. Mom was beside herself, sensing the tension but not knowing the cause. In the bathroom she pressed in. "What is going on?"

I knew we'd have to talk that day. I looked at Jenny, washing her hands. I would have loved to have spent the day alone with Jenny and Ben. When we got back to Aunt Vera's place, we'd have a little more privacy. "Mom, let's talk about this later."

She didn't want to be put off again. "No. Let's talk about whatever *it* is now so we can move on and enjoy the day. This is nonsense." She was mad. "Aunt Vera went out of her way to make this a special day for the family to have fun together, and so far we've been on opposite sides of the park."

She didn't have a clue. "Mom," I said, "this is about Nick. He's still doing the same things, but I don't want to talk about it here."

I'd said too much. Perplexed and furious, she was not going to wait. "Nick? What about Nick? Shelly, you never really let go of what happened. You're going to need to work this out or it's going to eat you up."

Now I was furious. I had compromised. I'd put up my walls to *protect* the integrity of the family, only to find out that he was doing the same things and more to others.

This was not about me. This was about Nick, and I was not going to cover it up this time. "No, Mom. You don't get it. It's not about me and old issues. We'll talk about it tonight."

Jenny watched our heated exchange. Her face was a mix of confusion and embarrassment. Here we were, in the ladies' room at Six Flags, about to hang our dirty laundry for all to see.

"No. We're gonna get this out right now." Mom was unrelenting.

Looking back, I see that Mom's anger was not directed at me. It was the fact that she couldn't see who or what she was fighting; but she knew she was in a fight.

Maybe she sensed—maybe we all sensed—the fight had been there all along, and now it was about to come to final blows.

"Mom, let's talk tonight. You don't want to do this now."

We walked out to where our group was. Mom had tears in her eyes —a mix of fear and confusion. She looked at me. "Yes, I do."

Everyone could see we were having a heated exchange. Mom informed the group we weren't doing anything till we cleared the air. "Shelly has something she needs to share." She looked at me. "Where do you want to go?"

There were people and tables all around us. "I don't want to do this. Not here." I looked at Marcy, Joey, and Aunt Vera. "We don't all need to be here."

By now Nick had an idea that he was at the core of the issue. I had barely looked at or spoken with him the last two days. I was shocked as he jumped in. "Why not? Shelly, if you've got an issue with me, then you tell it in front of everyone." It was a challenge I hadn't expected.

This time I wasn't bowing down. "Okay, let's go." We walked as a wary group to the park exit.

I had ignored Jesus for years, but I somehow knew that He would hear my prayers. I didn't have words, only a plea for help. Would *this* be the final straw to break Nick's back? What would the repercussions be? It didn't matter.

We found a grassy green belt and sat in a large circle. My heart felt as if it would pop out of my chest. I took a deep breath, hoping to ease it. I started with an apology to Aunt Vera. "This was supposed to be a special time for the family. I didn't plan on this, and I'm sorry."

I began to share. "Nick, you said if I had an issue with you, then share it with everyone . . . and I do. The issue is that you are doing things that are wrong and sick and illegal. You can't go on doing these things. Nick, what you did to me and what you are doing to others is just *wrong*."

Marcy's husband, Joey, didn't have any idea what I was speaking of. "Shelly, what are you talking about? What did he do to you?"

I hadn't considered that not everyone there that day knew what had happened. Even Ben and Jenny never really knew why we had gone to a shelter. "I'm talking about what happened years ago, when we ended up in a matter at court."

At that, Nick broke in. "Ah, geez." He looked at Joey. "All I did was . . ." He began to tell Joey about what happened the day after graduation.

At that, I sprang up and slapped him. "Don't you say another word. You *won't* go there again." No one had protected me then, and I was not going to be exposed again with his words. I was surprised at my boldness, but my heart was racing again.

"Nick, I know that you have been, *and are even still*, continuing to do these vile things. Hurting people. Hurting Marcy. And others, too."

Joey looked at Marcy, dumbfounded. Other family members, too, were in shock, trying to process what they were hearing.

Nick didn't deny any of it. He really didn't think what he did was wrong. That was the problem.

I finished as I faced Nick directly. "Nick, you have been part of my life for more than half of it. You've been good to us and cared for us, but you have a problem."

This should have been a private family discussion, but now it was out in the open. I looked at him one more time. "It's wrong, and I don't want anything to do with you anymore." I was fully convinced of my own words, but they stung even me as I spoke them. This was yet another relationship being cut. I walked away from the stunned circle.

As the words sank in, Mom began to crumble. She followed me as the shock gave way to words. "Shelly, I didn't know."

"Mom, it doesn't matter. You didn't protect me when you could have, and now it's led to more. I hate you for that."

She literally began to collapse before me. Ben was by her side. I didn't care. I was breaking away, and I wouldn't be brought back by an emotional outburst.

I walked to the end of the greenbelt. The sun was setting over the hills before me. I noted the beauty but was too numb to appreciate it.

I stood for a moment, voicing a prayer. This time I had words.

"Jesus, where do we go from here?"

If ever Nick was pushed to really lose it, surely this would be it. I considered him capable of taking my life and perhaps others. I wondered . . .

Will I see Brad and Jake again?

For the first time my anger had risen above my fear. I didn't care what followed. It was done.

The Great I AM peered over the crest of the hills. He looked at the man.

"I made you, son. The sickness of your lust and the disease of your mind are not from Me. I saw when you gave in and chose sin. You nursed lust until it became entangled in who I made you to be. Your lust has torn you; now it cuts and tears others from you. You are a sinner, and I sent My Son for you. One day you will call to Me, and I will answer. One day you will be free. Despite your wretchedness, I love you."

He looked to the wife.

"Daughter, you have forgotten me. It's been so long since you've sought My face. I see your sorrow. I see your loneliness. You are a sinner, and I sent My Son for you. One day you will turn back to me, and your joy will return. One day you will remember who I created you to be. Despite your blindness, I love you."

And finally, He looked at the young woman.

"Child, you run everywhere, but not to Me. When You do call to Me, you do not listen for My response. Be careful. Be very careful. I am not the only One jealous for you, and it is not the man who is your enemy. You have an unseen enemy who will relentlessly pursue you. You are a sinner, but I sent My Son for you. I have plans for you. One day you will see through My eyes.

"Despite your waywardness, I love you."

Home in California at last, I spent hours on the shore, gazing out to the sea. In exasperation, I grabbed fistfuls of sand and rocks, throwing them at the ocean. Like my response to reality, it was aimless and pointless.

Like the spray that rose with each crest of a wave, the Holy Spirit swept over the woman, offering fresh hope and truth continuously.

In the voice of the wind, the Great Shepherd called to the wandering lamb.

"You are at a precarious place on the side of the mountain. Follow My steps to peace and safety. It is a steep climb, but I will anchor you. If you reach to anything but Me, you will be led onto paths that will take you where you do not want to go.

"You will feel the cords of temptation wrapped around you like a harness. The cords will feel secure. You'll be drawn to grasp and cleave to judgment, anger, and unforgiveness. They will only tangle and ensnare you further. Bitterness will offer a foothold to brace you, but it is poison that will seep into your innermost being; it will cause your heart to become hard and cold. You'll find sympathy in the arms of pity and comfort in worldly justifications. But these will never bring healing. You'll be drawn to things that numb your pain. Don't buy it! It's nothing more than slow death.

"Your path has not been easy, but the one you are about to take is costly.

First, it will lure you. Then, it will trap you. Next, it will strangle the life you have. Finally, it will shape you into a twisted form of what I created you to be.

"Child, hear My voice! I am jealous for you."

As long as you hold on to the hurts of the past, your past has a grip on you. I became consumed with the past and its shattered dreams. Jesus could have—would have—helped. But as soon as I called out to Jesus, I had then promptly turned the other way.

When I returned from St. Louis, the walls I had so neatly built around my heart crumbled, imploding inward. I spiraled back into the dark, lonely pit I had been in back at the shelter. Full of anger and resentment, I cut off all contact with both Mom and Nick. I wanted nothing more to do with them.

I had one last discussion with Mom, telling her such. "If there's family business I need to know, you can pass it along through Brad or Miss Toni." That was it. Our communication ended there.

I sought professional help but, really, I was looking for a credible source to validate that my life officially stunk.

Once I started on the introspective path, I became self-centered and fell deeper into a dark pit of misery. Brad was ill-equipped to help me. He had his own issues and didn't know what to do. But he stayed with me. Jake was the one good and bright spot in our lives.

As I focused on what was behind me, I found it more difficult to disassociate the darkness of the past from my challenges in the present. My emotional frustration began to twist and spill over into physical intimacy with Brad. It was easier just to pull away entirely.

Sorrow, rejection and shame can cut and injure people deeper than physical wounds can; however, greater injury occurs when one allows these to take over his or her identity.

Acquainted with His daughter's pain, the Father beckoned. "Turn to Me."

For years, growing up, I'd had trouble sleeping. I would wake up from vivid dreams of Nick chasing me, seeking my life for revenge for disrupting his. The dreams lessened when I left home, but now the nightmares returned with a vengeance.

I went to counseling, which led to more questions, more introspection, and more depression. It also led us to financial debt.

Besides counseling, I tried self-help books, antidepressants, palm reading, and "inner child" healing. I grasped at anything that could fix me—except Jesus.

"I am Your counselor. I alone have what you need."

I went to an inpatient program for adult survivors of childhood sexual abuse. Soon, I was more confused, more self-focused, and on stronger antidepressants.

From there, I joined a support group for women who had gone through the same things.

"This counsel is stirring contention, fear, hostility. Depart from it. Turn to Me and see that My wisdom heals."

I became close with a few sex abuse survivors, and too close with one in particular. I didn't see it as an unhealthy relationship, but it was.

"Do not be foolish child. Wake up!"

I met Zoe in our support group. We began to spend more time together. We related at a deep level, and we had fun together. She had a background similar to mine and understood me in a way Brad couldn't.

As I lost connection with my husband, I gained connection with Zoe.

I knew Brad was frustrated. He desired physical intimacy but withheld emotional intimacy. I desired emotional intimacy but felt exposed with physical intimacy. We were messed up, and our marriage and marriage bed were neither safe nor appealing.

While we tried different ways to fix our brokenness, we inched our way toward divorce. We were spinning in circles, getting nowhere. We had no vision, so we had no hope.

I shared with Zoe that I struggled with physical intimacy with Brad. I asked her, "What if I never want to be physically intimate with Brad or any man again? Will it always take me back to thoughts of Nick?"

I couldn't stand the thought of physical intimacy, but I didn't want to be alone either. My mind began to entertain thoughts of what life would look like if . . .

It wasn't about sex; it was about intimacy.

I shared my considerations with my counselor and with Zoe. My counselor suggested I journal my thoughts. "It may help you process."

Zoe agreed. She had done the same thing and found it helpful. I got a journal and wrote my thoughts out, exploring the possibilities of what an *alternative* relationship would look like.

I wrote and explored and wrote some more. I fantasized on paper, considering what a lesbian lifestyle would be like. I reasoned, *There . . . it's out. That should lessen its power.*

But in reality, the idea grew and took greater occupancy in my thought life.

I talked with my counselor about what I was considering. I also talked about it with Zoe. She understood. The more I talked about it, the more I entertained it.

In some remote part of my mind a voice continued warning me: *"You are being deceived."*

I didn't hear the words, but nuances of God's truths sifted through my thoughts. The beautiful, faraway voice only aggravated me. I had tried being the good girl—the peacemaker. I had been the one to compromise. I had given my best.

One evening I came home from the grocery store. Something was wrong. Brad looked at me with eyes that seemed to see right through me. I squirmed with guilt.

"What's wrong?" I asked him.

He pointed to the table. "I read it."

There laid my journal. I was immediately angry and defensive, but then I saw the pain in his eyes as he asked, "So that's how you feel? Not even another man, but a *woman*?"

I didn't know what to say. In fact, I don't remember any words that followed that night. The only thing I do remember is what happened the next morning.

Brad had woken up early as usual to make the long drive to his account downtown. He was in the shower. I lay beneath the white cotton comforter, wanting to hide forever.

I heard him weep. I'd never even seen him cry. Then I heard a thud as his body slumped to the floor in the steamy shower, weeping more.

I had caused this. I couldn't undo it. I hated myself. He didn't deserve this. I couldn't take back the words.

Why is this happening?

I would have liked to disappear forever except for the little boy asleep in his new big-boy bed.

I hated my life. I had become someone I'd never thought I'd be. That should have been the end of a destructive season, but it wasn't.

The jealous King watched the battle as the enemy closed in, circling his prey.

"Daughter, don't you see? You are dancing with your opponent."

I didn't question *if* God was out there. Even in the darkness, I occasionally sensed His presence. When He came to mind, my anger burned. My heart had grown bitter toward Him.

How could He sit by and watch me and countless others go through these kinds of things?

I wanted nothing to do with Him.

He would not pluck her against her will out of the deep, dark, muddy pit. But the Holy Spirit remained continuously before her. "Stubborn child, you cannot wander so far that My love will not reach further. I will pursue you."

In 1993 the large systems computer industry began to change. This was Brad's business, and when the industry changed, so did Brad's accounts. He was offered more money to help out an account in Dallas, Texas.

Neither of us had ever been to Texas nor desired to go there.

A bunch of cowboys and no beach? Yeah, right. No thanks.

But when the offer came around again, we were deep in debt. It seemed our best option. For Brad it also meant separation from our messed-up lives. For me it was change. I was desperate for it.

I called Zoe to let her know we were moving. With the news, she shared that she thought we had more than a friendship. Maybe we had a future together. Could I really move and leave her so easily? She suggested we meet for dinner.

What?!

I didn't realize she saw our relationship that way. My head spun.

I pondered what she said, and then I did the worst thing possible. I entertained further thoughts and possibilities—as if I had not done enough damage!

As Brad and I wrestled with our falling-apart marriage, I began to consider how I would provide for myself and Jake if Brad and I divorced. Jake was the brightest part of life. To provide for our own place and child care, I would have to go back to work.

I didn't have a college education and only limited experience in the banking industry. Modeling days were long gone. The only value I thought I had was my appeal to the opposite sex. I reasoned that if it came down to it, I could make money if I sold myself.

How does one get started? I wondered. I took notice of women who looked like they might be in the "industry" in case I needed to explore options.

I had connected with Zoe, but I had not considered it physical. When Zoe expressed an interest in a long-term relationship, I saw an opportunity. Maybe I wouldn't have to take an unsavory job. Zoe would understand and help. I could work part-time at a bank and go to school.

Would I dare to share my thoughts with her? I was about to find out.

A few days later, we met for dinner near her place. I was scared and desperate and stupid. I wanted some kind of solution. A part of me didn't want to cross the line; another part (with a loud voice of desperation) saw the dismal reality right in front of me.

Life isn't working out the way it is, maybe this is better.

We were in a parking garage when Zoe invited me to her apartment. The knot in my stomach should have been a warning to run the other way. I contemplated. Then I stalled.

I don't know if I can do this.

I squirmed inside with unease and stalled further. Zoe said something I knew I'd heard before. "You don't know till you try."

Who'd said that?

I tried to remember when I'd heard that last.

Brad was on call around the clock, with a two-hour response. We lived a good hour away from downtown. He had given me his pager in case he got paged.

In the midst of my contemplating, the pager went off. I was twenty minutes from home. I called Brad to let him know.

"Okay, Shelly. You need to get home now."

Relief swept over me, but the heaviness of what I had just contemplated weighed me down. "Zoe, I have to go."

I sped home so Brad could head downtown and I could be home with Jake. Despite my guilt and waywardness, I saw Jake as a little beacon of light and purity. Somehow his presence offered hope and a future, though I couldn't understand it.

When I got to the condo, Brad called the branch manager to let him know he was on his way.

"What for?" the manager said. "Everything's running fine."

Brad told him a service call had been placed and read him the problem code, to which the manager replied, "There must have been some fluke in the system; the person who placed the call isn't even here anymore."

I knew something exceptional had happened, but I wasn't willing to face God at that point.

His anger shot out like lightning in the spring sky. His sorrow filled the clouds with heavy rain. "You are just like my beloved Israel—obstinate—choosing to follow your own ways!"

We eventually made our way to Dallas. I left Zoe with a promise to keep in touch. She talked about coming out to see me and picking up from there. Gratefully, she didn't, and the relationship fizzled. My dirty little secret remained hidden.

As soon as we found an apartment, I set out to find a new counselor and psychiatrist. I wanted someone to refill my antidepressant prescription and someone who would give me one of those long psych evaluations to diagnose me. Then we could work on the cure. I found someone who would do both.

We set one appointment for the test day and another two weeks later for the results review. Ms. Carlson had a beautiful office with fine furnishings. It was elegant yet inviting. Her office suite reflected her style: sophisticated and cultured. I was pumped that someone qualified was going to remedy my dilemma.

The test made my head spin. It was loaded with questions that were repeated and reworded. It was long, and my brain was fried trying to figure out how to answer.

When it came time for the results, I sat in a soft leather chair facing her. I was eager to hear her findings.

Finally, a breakthrough. We're going to make headway here!

She looked at me with a meager smile and a question in her eyes. "Are you ready?"

I guessed she was curious at my excitement, but I had waited so long to find out what was wrong with me and how it could be fixed!

She politely told me she had gathered and reviewed the results. She'd had another colleague review the results as well, and she shared with their conclusion: Their evaluation? "You will always struggle with depression."

Did she say "always"? But I'm only depressed because I don't know what's wrong with me!

"I'm afraid it's in your genes," she said, looking over her glasses as she switched from reading her notes to looking at me.

This wasn't what I was hoping for. "My *genes*?" I took a deep breath. "What do you mean?"

She sat tall and leaned toward me in her chair. "It means you will always struggle with depression." She continued, "You will always need to be on medication, and because medications only work for a time, they will need to be changed from time to time and the potency increased."

She's said always three times. Whoa. This is a death sentence.

I stared back at her, perplexed. "Really?"

She politely nodded. "Yes, I'm afraid so. But we can work together to manage it well, and you can live a reasonably normal life."

Numbly, I listened, thanked her, and left.

I'd hit a wall. It was painful to hear. She was fully convinced of her words. She didn't ask if I agreed with her. Why would she? She was the professional.

It hit me hard and woke me up.

"I have given you the gift of choice. Are you really going to allow a stranger, professional or not, to dictate what the rest of your life is going to look like?

"I am your God; you shall have no other."

I didn't want to live the life Ms. Carlson described. I drove to an empty parking lot to process all she'd said.

All the counseling, groups, and introspection had been a dismal failure. I was no better off for the time and money Brad and I had spent. In truth we were worse off.

I didn't return to Ms. Carlson, or any counselor, and I stopped taking antidepressants that day.

Now understand: I *never* recommend anyone go off meds like that. It's stupid and can be dangerous. I was just ignorant enough not to care and was very fortunate not to have any problems.

"She does not recognize My voice yet."

The Protector saw the snare his daughter had just escaped. He loathed the pop culture that thrived on pharmaceutical dependency and earthly knowledge in place of His truth and power.

"Enter through the narrow gate," He had written, "for the gate is wide and the way is broad that leads to destruction, and there are many who enter through it" (Matthew 7:13).

Brad was immersed in his work, so I decided to find work of my own where I could make an impact seeing justice served.

I took a position as an intern with a crime scene investigation lab. I loved that everything was black-and-white. I found there is always a trail of truth, though it may be hidden or unseen. It was always there, could always be found; you just had to search for it.

We processed through evidence and found facts; however, it wasn't the truth I was looking for. I needed more.

At one point we worked a capital murder case involving the death of a young child. It was a tough case to process, but it served as another wake-up call. I had my own child, with whom I could be spending time and attention.

I stepped down from my role so I could give my full attention to Jake. He was the one perfect spot in our lives—if I missed out on being his mom, I would have nothing left.

9

THE ENCOUNTER

*B*rad and I were now in debt financially, relationally, and spiritually. We really didn't even have a true marriage. We were more like roommates, having given up on both physical and emotional intimacy.

We were the epitome of the living dead; we were zombies before zombies were "in." There's really nothing cool about rotting flesh carrying around a bunch of old garbage. It just really stinks.

We were good friends, but we were miserable. We agreed to give our marriage six more months. If we didn't make headway, we would proceed toward separation. Six months came and went, but neither of us were willing to leave Jake. We gave it another three months, then another.

Jake was four when we moved into a condo in Plano, Texas. It was winter 1994. I loved our second-story condo. It was spacious with a view of greens and trees—a great place for Jake to run and play.

That spring, new neighbors moved into the vacant condo next door. Suzie was a single mom with two kids, Sarah and Matthew. Matthew and Jake were six months apart. They became inseparable, and our two families became close.

At that time, I still had no contact with Mom. I only knew she had divorced Nick shortly after the St. Louis incident.

If she called, Brad would talk to her and let her know how Jake was doing. Mostly, she and I spoke to Toni, who kept common contact between us. She called Brad in April to let us know Ben's childhood friend John had died from a moped accident.

What? No!

My heart sank.

Seriously, God?

John and Ben had been as close as brothers since grade school. John had come with us on vacations and had become an endearing part of the family. He understood our family dynamics and was great at breaking up the tension with his sense of humor and mischief. He and Ben were roommates after high school. The two had come out to see us in California. They did life together.

God, how could You?!

Ben is one of the kindest souls I know. Hadn't he been through enough with Nick? John's untimely death poured more gas on the fire of my anger toward God.

I went to Phoenix for the funeral. I wanted to honor John's family, but I especially wanted to be there for Ben. I could only imagine how hard this hit him. John had been loved by everyone, but he was Ben's soul mate. This would be one of the toughest blows he'd faced.

Brad's sister, Theresa, picked me up from the airport, and I stayed with Momma Ruth. I hadn't seen my Mom since St. Louis. She would be at the service, and I would be polite, but I had no reason to pursue a relationship. I knew my heart was cold, but I rationalized. *It's safer this way.*

I found a place to sit next to Jenny at the ceremony. Looking around the large room, I was surprised to see so many people wearing bright-colored clothes instead of black. *That's weird.*

Jenny and I sat quietly, watching. In my mind I looked back over the years, thinking about John and how he'd make us laugh.

Weren't we just kids, with John doing his fake fart impressions?

I could hear John's roaring laughter as we ducked oncoming waves on the shore at Seal Beach not so long ago.

When the music began, I was confused. There was a band.

Oh, this is bad. Somebody messed up royal. Do they even know this is a funeral?

I looked at Jenny, raising my eyebrows.

As I studied her beautiful almond eyes it struck me: *Wow, Jen's not a kid anymore. She really is a beautiful young woman. And she's so smart. Oh, how I love this girl.*

The music grew louder.

But what is up with this music?

Then I listened to the words. It was a homecoming celebration. The song spoke of saints in heaven welcoming John to his final destination, his true home. Heaven.

Something stirred deep inside me as I squirmed, suddenly uneasy in my seat. It was the seed my friend Chip had planted years before. I didn't recognize it through my hostility toward God.

The Lamb's Book. I wasn't ready to face it; but something was happening, and I couldn't stop it.

I returned to Dallas and found Jake full of questions.

"What happens when you die?"

"Where does your body go?"

"What is heaven?"

"Do bad guys go to heaven?"

His faint brows crinkled as his eyes opened wide with each question. I attempted to answer his questions. He wanted to know more about God. The more he talked about God, the more he lit up.

That week little Matthew asked if Jake could come to church with him. Suzie asked me if Jake could join them and suggested Brad and I come too.

Neither Brad nor I had any intention of doing the church scene, but the timing was convenient with Jake asking all his God questions. We agreed to check it out for Jake's sake.

Jake continued to want to know more about the invisible God. "How do you know He's there if you can't see Him?"

Good question, Jake.

My inner hostility toward God intensified as Jake's hunger to know about Him increased. It was as if God were invading our home, and He was using our son.

Suzie invited us to her Wednesday night small group. "We can take the kids to children's class," she said. I hesitated. Suzie squeezed my arm and laughed. "Come on. It's really casual. You'll like it, and the kids always have fun."

Brad and I agreed. "We should go back so he can get the right answers from someone who knows better than us," we told each other We knew we were the last ones to be telling him about God.

Suzie was right. The people were normal. They welcomed us without expectations. We didn't share our problems, though the evening always ended with prayer. When they asked us how they could pray for us specifically, we only shared surface needs.

As we continued to attend church and Suzie's small group, I inwardly became more agitated. I couldn't figure out what was going on. I liked the people, but the whole *God part* stirred up my deep, hidden struggle.

I didn't want to think about Him.

I didn't want to face Him.

I did not want anything to do with the God who simply allowed shameless things to happen when He had the power to do something.

Now He seemed to be crowding in around us. It was as if He were pursuing us. Jake couldn't stop talking about Him, and I couldn't escape, nor could I deny Him.

Why?!

How could He be so good and holy in the church but let so many harsh things happen outside of it? Why hadn't He intervened when *I* needed Him?

Where was He when I was rejected and left alone?

What kind of a God lets His children suffer?

Who takes mothers and fathers and children before their time?

I hated Him.

"Enough, child! Face Me! See WHO I AM."

Brad and I had a small tiff. It was one among countless others, but it was the one that pushed me over the top.

Brad wasn't the issue.

I was so tired of fighting just to breathe the breath of life. I resented seeing Jesus answer prayers all around me. He even answered some of our courtesy prayers as we dabbled in prayer with our new church friends. We weren't about to share what was *really* going on in our lives.

How dare God answer our little prayers when we were suffocating, even hemorrhaging, inside!

I did not get on my knees. I did not bow my head.

I slammed the door, locked myself in the bedroom, flung my fists in the air, and started yelling at God.

"Why don't YOU just do something with my life and my marriage? I don't want it! I can't leave it. I've screwed it up so bad. Just take it! You know what? I don't think You can, 'cause You haven't done a damn thing so far!"

I fumed on, blood boiling. I was so mad, so hating God, and so alone. But for the first time maybe ever, I was truly addressing Him stripped down to who I really was. I wanted to punch Him and kick Him. Why was He so *invisible*?!

"I can't even see You!"

I ranted on and wept until I was absolutely empty.

Silent moments followed. Alone in the bedroom, I was aware of only a profound silence.

There was nothing left of me. It was as if I finally broke when I turned to fully, truly *face* him.

Suddenly, my mind's eyes took me beyond the bedroom. Pieces of me lay broken and strewn about. The ugliness of all that was within me poured out upon the floor. Then, the King of Kings pierced through the darkness, revealing His presence in words of life:

"I'm here."

It was beyond audible—more than mere words—it was *His presence.*

The King was *present,* there *before* me, more real than my raw emptiness.

It was as though I had awakened from a dream to reality. Cognizant of Him, my soul breathed in the peace of His existence. I had never been more at home, more complete, than in that moment, fully aware of the *presence* of the King.

It was a moment, or perhaps a set of moments, that will last in my mind forever. I could barely stand to look upon His splendor.

Jesus. The King. Full of Glory.

In His brilliant light, all deception was exposed.

I saw myself, a sinner, embodied in the ugliness of my own despicable sin.

It was as if I were made of stone: hard and disfigured. I lay in dry, broken pieces before the Great King, while His glory and radiance pulsed with power.

Anger, fear, judgment, bitterness, and unforgiveness . . . my sin had reshaped me into a miserable, distorted version of His original design.

I had become blind without vision and disconnected from the vibrancy of life. I wore a dark cloak and a crown of shame.

Instead of running with life, I had been pitifully crawling on mangled limbs.

It was both a horrific sight and one of wonder all at once. Bowing before Him, illuminated in His light, I understood.

He is worthy of life and glory and honor and worship.

He is to be adored and revered.

There before me stood the Creator, dazzling like the stars, luminescent like the moon, and shining like the sun. Light, like countless diamonds and flickering jewels, danced before my mind's eye.

His beauty is breathtaking. The contrast between me and Him, immeasurable. In His presence I understood: He has made all things to *reflect* and *magnify* Him.

And I was not who He'd created me to be.

Two words came out of me, though I couldn't tell whether they came from my lips or somewhere deep inside: "Jesus . . . Worthy."

It was as if those words explained my entire life—had been there all along, and I had missed them.

I wept, broken before the King, grieving at what I had become and how I had whored myself out to other gods, denying the one true living God.

His eyes did not disagree, nor did they condemn. They blazed with holy fire. I dared not look away.

He spoke. *"You are mine, child."*

His words were living color—rich and vibrant, casting light upon me, the tones and inflections a symphony of perfection, both elegant and powerful. They struck my innermost being much the way the sight of a tree flush with fall's brilliant yellow and crimson stirs one's very soul. His voice carried like thunder yet soothed like a long-awaited rain in the parched desert.

He continued to cast missiles of holy fire. *"I love you."*

When He spoke, His words took flight. Each word was a beautiful, living jewel that lifted and carried life. Each word was like an arrow, landing with precision and cutting through to the marrow of my bones.

His words were *alive!*

The prick and sting of these penetrating words was exquisite; the impartation was eternal hope. He had called me "Mine"! His words astounded me.

This was different from someone telling me, "Jesus loves you." The King Himself was imparting life into me with His words.

He smiled and sighed. His very breath, like eagle's wings, rose toward the heavens and descended like a dove lighting.

The Holy One extended His hand. *"Come."*

In awe and trepidation, I drew near.

Tenderly, He removed from me the heavy, bloodstained cloak of darkness that embodied all that had been done to me. I realized I'd felt that same kindness decades ago in Dad as we held the dying bird in our hands.

"Jesus, You were there!"

He threw His head back and laughed. *"Daughter, I have always been right here."*

I was taken by His laughter. Laughter from the Mighty King?

Yes, laughter! It was full and booming, shaking me to my core. It provoked a deep hunger to hear more.

I was stunned at every aspect of Him.

My senses came awake as if for the first time. I smelled a familiar scent—like the ocean's morning mist and fresh jasmine.

"Jesus, You were there—the gardenias by Momma Ruth's door, and You were there on the path I run. And . . ."

His smile burned brightly. Liquid love shimmered in His words. *"Yes, child. I've always been here, right beside you, wherever you are."*

I tried to take it all in. The King was before me, and He'd been there all my days—everywhere.

It was so much to take in.

The grandeur of His presence overwhelmed me. Though in a state of awe, I recognized that His presence was my true HOME.

He's always been here!

Patiently He watched as I tried to grasp the reality of Him:

His presence was a constant flow of moving light, color, scent, sound, energy.

His beauty was indescribable and intoxicating.

His power . . . majestic.

His words . . . piercing.

"I love you, child."

His presence was weighty with authority, commanding honor and the deepest veneration.

He is a fierce Warrior with an arsenal of immeasurable power, the depths of which no human mind can conceive. He exudes sovereignty over the universe and every living thing therein!

I trembled before the Almighty One.

He sees all. There is nothing He does not see.

He is before me, but He's all around me without end.

He is always there—everywhere.

I shuddered at the thought of my wretchedness in His presence as I lay before Him bare, flesh rotting with the disease of my sin. I realized the stench of it.

Sin had eaten at my flesh and distorted His design. My grief was great.

"Lord, what have I done?" I knew then my greatest sin was forsaking His presence.

"I am sorry, Lord."

Surely I was too far gone to have any worth to Him. What had I done to His creation of me?

Yet here He was, right before me.

My eyes were open, and He was all I wanted.

He bent down and gathered my brokenness. He moved like a tremendous fire.

I burned in His hands, yet without pain. His touch was strong and electric, sure and healing.

At first, the disease of my sin, exposed in His light, appeared as if it began at the surface and corrupted inwardly. But then Jesus reached inside me and took my heart.

My *heart* was the source of my disease—my sin.

It was like a cancer: cold and deformed, consuming though lacking life. It was bound in black cords of unforgiveness that spliced into veins, bleeding the poison that fed my disease.

He took my wretched heart—and placed it in His chest!

"Nooo!"

Appalled, I willed my hands to take it back though I could barely move. It was polluted, diseased, infectious, and shameful. The inferior heart belonged in my disgusting, corrupt shell, not His perfect form.

"Surely you will give me your heart," He said gently.

The sight of Him . . . Pure. Holy. Magnificent and glorious—taking my corroded heart in Him. I was undone.

"Yes, Lord."

> *Bless the LORD, O my soul . . . who pardons all your iniquities,*
> *who heals all your diseases; who redeems your life from the*
> *pit, who crowns you with lovingkindness and compassion.*
> —*Psalm 103:1–4*

But He was not finished.

With His other hand, He placed a piece of His own heart in my chest!

Too much. This is too much.

No words could convey the magnitude of His great benevolence.

His compassion was uncontainable light and power, stirring intensely with the vibrancy of life. I shook violently within.

"Oh, Great King . . . Jesus."

Then I realized—the fierce tremble was His heart beating within me.

"I will give you a new heart and put a new spirit within you," He said, *"and I will remove the heart of stone from your flesh and give you a heart of flesh"* (Ezekiel 36:26).

It could have been a millennium or a suspended moment. Time. Didn't. Matter.

My Lord waited as I grasped the greatness of what He had done.

And the greatness of who He is. Suddenly, a prayer rose up within me:

> *Create in me a clean heart, O God,*
> *And renew a steadfast spirit within me.*
> *Do not cast me away from Your presence*
> *And do not take Your Holy Spirit from me.*
> *Restore to me the joy of Your salvation*
> *And sustain me with a willing spirit.*
> *Then I will teach transgressors Your ways,*
> *And sinners will be converted to You.* (Psalm 51:10–13)

I looked upon the Great King, shining in the splendor of His glory. He placed a garment of pure white upon me. Bowed low and weeping still, I feared that I would defile His garment.

"What could You have to do with one as lowly as me?"

But as my tears fell, soaking me and the clean garment with repentance, the garment became a healing cloth upon me.

His righteous covering absolved my disease.

His heart within me pumped His lifeblood throughout my being. A glistening stream of hope pervaded the dark places within, further awakening my innermost being.

The Savior touched my face—the most tender touch a soul could hope to know. It was as though I FELT for the first time.

Kindness. Grace. Holy acceptance.

At once my rotting flesh began to heal and transform. My crown of shame fell at His feet.

He touched the scars of my past and smiled with ancient wisdom. Tracing each scar with His gaze, He left them in place and sealed them with more living words.

"These will shine with evidence of My redemption and My glory."

Slowly, He lifted my hand to help me rise.

His touch was thrilling, pulsing holy fire.

New life coursed through my veins as I stood, unable to take my eyes off Him.

What had been dark, diseased, disfigured, and broken was now whole. My scars remained, but now laced with translucent gold, revealing what was within: hope and the light of His glory and redemption. Joy soared upward as I rose.

He looked into my eyes. The beauty of His grace and kindness captivated me.

He extended His mighty hand, resting it upon my head. Fire lit within my bones.

"You are Mine," He said. *"I have crowned you with grace. Do you understand? You are Mine. Now, follow Me."*

At last, I became aware of my physical self and my surroundings. It hadn't been a dream, but now I was fully awake—fully ALIVE.

Jesus became my reality.

I had not seen this with my physical eyes. This was different—far richer. I had seen with the eyes of my heart and mind.

The impression left an impact that forever changed me.

One cannot undo what the presence of the Lord has done.

He absolved my disease.

He called me HIS.

I had His heart and lifeblood pumping in me.

And I had seen Jesus.

Jesus the Kinsman-Redeemer.

Jesus the Savior.

Jesus the King.

That was the day I began to truly understand love. Not only had I fallen into the presence of true love, but the King would teach *me* to love. It was then I realized that the gift God gave us in Jake had been a bigger gift in passing on the hope of the light of Christ Jesus.

I still had much to learn, but on that day I woke up and saw the Lord. The trajectory of my life changed. I was awake and alive and truly began to live.

My circumstances didn't change, yet everything was different. I was not void of the sin nature, but it no longer controlled me. I had the presence and power of Christ *inside* me.

I had experienced the *presence* of God. I had tasted of His goodness, and I wanted more.

Each day that followed, I looked for practical direction from Jesus. I found it in the Bible and time in prayer.

It wasn't about fixing my marriage. It wasn't about being free from my past. It wasn't even about my future. I simply wanted to know Jesus more.

I became a student of Christ, looking for Him, learning from Him, and following His ways. I couldn't get enough of Him.

At first, when I took a few steps, I would look to Him, expecting to be finished. "Okay, done."

Then He would beckon me further, *"Follow Me,"* revealing another step.

The stories in the Bible came alive. I saw myself *in* His stories.

The person and character of Jesus crystalized as I read the Gospels.

Matters that had previously perplexed me were now clear and under-standable.

I pitched a tent in Psalm 23 and devoured Proverbs. Paul's letter to the Romans painted a picture tying the Old and New Testaments together in one massive mural of all time.

The more I spent time studying the King, the more I fell in love with Him. He consumed my thoughts and changed the way I thought. I started to see life and people differently.

I began to learn how to truly love people, starting with my husband.

The Lord led me on a path taking steps that were tough. That meant giving myself physically and emotionally to Brad at *his* point of desire. It was really uncomfortable to start, but as soon as I took action, not only did He provide me the ability to do what He called me to; He provided peace and pleasure.

The apostle Paul said, "Not that we are adequate in ourselves to consider anything as coming from ourselves, but our adequacy is from God" (2 Corinthians 3:5).

I found this to be true.

As Brad and I continued to follow Christ's ways, our marriage changed. I found satisfaction serving and caring for Brad over myself. Intimacy took on a whole new meaning. I saw that I had held a warped understanding of physical and emotional intimacy connected to my past. I had been as absent sexually as Brad had been emotionally.

God gave Brad patience and me grace to untangle the pieces connected to old wounds. In time we found the marriage bed not only safe, but sacred, satisfying, and desirable.

Our lives changed radically, but God is never finished with us. He pressed on.

Follow Me.

10

ON SOLID GROUND

*P*aul's letter to the Ephesians served as a great tool to hammer out the kinks in Brad's heart and mine. This verse in particular spoke to us:

> You were taught, with regard to your former way of life, to put
> off your old self, which is being corrupted by its deceitful
> desires; to be made new in the attitude of your minds; and
> to put on the new self, created to be like God in true
> righteousness and holiness. (Ephesians 4:22–24 NIV)

Paul even gave specifics of what that should look like:

> Get rid of all bitterness, rage and anger . . . Be kind and
> compassionate to one another, forgiving each other, just as
> in Christ God forgave you. (Ephesians 4:31–32 NIV)

The more I studied God's Word, the more I perceived His voice.
"You have unfinished business, child."
I know, Lord. Where do we start?

He was talking about family. I understood He wanted to be the only thing between me and each member of our family: specifically, Momma Ruth. Mom. Dad. Nick.

Okay. Momma Ruth—that's easy.

There was only goodness between me and Momma Ruth, but did she know Jesus? We'd never really talked about Him before. I knew she knew *of* Him, but did she *know* Him?

If there was unfinished business with Momma Ruth, it was surely that He wanted me to share with her all the good things He was doing in us. I wrote to her, telling her how much our lives had changed because of Him. That would be a first step. I hoped Momma Ruth would weigh the words of the letter, and then we could go from there.

Then there was Mom.

Okay Jesus. Help me here.

I had cut Mom off and abandoned our relationship entirely. There was nothing there. I had been cold and callous toward her, depriving her of any part in our family. For over two years I had not spoken to or had anything to do with my mom.

But now grudges, estrangement, and unforgiveness had no room in my life. It did not match Who I belonged to.

"Freely you have received, freely give. As I love you, so you love others."

After all that Christ had done for me, who was I to withhold anything from Mom or Dad or Nick? I no longer wanted to withhold anything.

Christ's heart in me was much larger than my own. His lifeblood cleansed the corrosion of unforgiveness deposited by injustice, pain, rejection, anger, judgment, and hatred. All were washed away as His heart pumped life and forgiveness in place of the blockages within me.

Forgiveness didn't end with me being forgiven. In fact, that's when I began to forgive—*giving forth* that which I had been given but hadn't deserved.

Mom embraced me with open arms.

Dad . . .

Lord, You know I love him. What do I do?

"Daughter, you have much growing to do here. Just reach out and let him know you love him. Include him in your life. This will take time, but watch; I will do a new thing. You will see him as I do."

And Nick.

Lord?

I had forgiven him, but I knew Christ wanted more. Nick needed more than a "cure" for his sickness. He needed the love of Christ.

I sent a letter to Nick, sharing openly and honestly without diminishing what he had done, but rather, offering words of grace, forgiveness and hope.

One day soon after that, I came home from a jog. Jake was next door, at Matthew's. Brad was sitting on the floor, staring out the window. I could tell something was wrong. I unlaced my shoes. "Hey. You okay?"

He didn't say anything but shook his head, continuing to look out the window.

"Brad?" I went and sat beside him, touching his arm. I waited. "Hey . . ."

I could see he was struggling to get words out. I put my hand on his and waited. He broke his gaze and dropped his face down. "Momma Ruth is gone."

Gone? Now I was speechless. I looked at him as he snatched a grief-filled glance at me and looked away again. He choked on his words. "Sis called. Mom had a heart attack. Sis found her too late."

We sat together in silence and disbelief. We both had the same unspoken question.

Did she know Him?

The Shepherd grieved with His two children.
In the quiet stillness, they were aware of His presence.

We flew to Phoenix for the funeral. It was bittersweet. We cried and laughed, reflecting on good times and memories. Along with Brad and his siblings, I, too, would be missing Momma Ruth greatly.

Momma Ruth had made a place for me in her life. She accepted me as I was, with no strings attached. She had been a safe haven when Brad and I separated and I needed a place to simply *be*.

When I had severed ties with my mom, Momma Ruth didn't judge me or try to fix me. She didn't prod or get in my business. She simply welcomed me to be with her. I would miss our hours of puzzles and TV and chattering about unimportant things. We'd spent a lot of time together just enjoying each other's company.

As we packed up special mementos and reminisced, Brad and I considered that we did not know whether or not Momma Ruth had walked with Christ.

I hadn't outright asked Momma Ruth if she really knew Jesus after I sent the letter. I wished I had.

Momma Ruth's passing was a rude awakening. You never know what may be someone's last day. And what if you are God's plan to share the truth with that person before that day comes? It was a sobering thought.

No one likes to think that someone they love may not be in heaven or may not be going there. If God is good and heaven is a place for good people . . .

But Jesus said, "I am the way and the truth and the life. No one comes to the Father except through me" (John 14:6 NIV).

We knew "good" isn't good enough. God sent Jesus to live and die and rise again to make way for all to enter heaven. He did it for all, but not all will enter—only those who accept the gift of life eternal by faith in Him.

It made me think of races I'd run. Most anyone can run. Just because someone runs doesn't mean he is in a race. You have to register with the registrar. Once your name is registered, you receive an entry. You have your own unique identity within the race . . . bib number 1132. There's a specific route to run.

Nor can you win a prize because others think you're a good runner. You have to show up to the race. No matter how good you are or how much others love you, sideline cheers won't place you in the winner's circle.

And for certain no one else can run your race for you. The apostle Paul made this clear: "Do you not know that those who run in a race all run, but only one receives the prize? Run in such a way that you may win" (1 Corinthians 9:24).

Jake was about to turn five when he began praying for a baby brother or sister for his birthday. It didn't happen for his birthday, but we joined his prayers asking God for another child.

We were elated when I became pregnant soon after that. We gave the baby a name and began making plans. I was sure this child was also a boy.

Brad came with me to meet our new OB-GYN. We were both surprised she wanted to do a sonogram so early (I was well into the second semester before we had one with Jake). Nothing was wrong, but technology was advancing, and we were ready to see our next new baby.

Brad was holding my hand when the doctor told us our baby was no longer living. I was only three months along. Brad's grip tightened and our hearts broke. We had never considered the possibility of miscarriage.

How do we explain this to a five-year-old who's been praying for a brother or sister?

We cried together as a family for the loss of the dream we'd prayed for.

My close friend Kathy, who was also pregnant, kept Jake at her house for a sleepover when I went in for the D&C. When I saw Kathy at church the next day, she came into our class round with child and dressed entirely in black—the kindness of Christ personified in a true friend. She was the very embodiment of the verse "Rejoice with those who rejoice, and weep with those who weep" (Romans 12:15).

A couple of months later, I was pregnant again. This time we waited longer to tell Jake. I marked off the calendar week by week, waiting for a thumbs-up from the doctor.

One day while Brad was working, Jake and I ran errands. We were driving when I noticed an exceptionally large and fluffy dandelion off the side of the road. I pulled onto the shoulder in the middle of nowhere.

Jake looked at me quizzically as we got out of the car. "Why'd you stop, Mom? There's nothing here."

I plucked the giant wildflower and handed it to him. "It's a wishing flower, and this one is special because it's so huge."

I explained how we used to blow on them and make a wish when we were kids. He looked at me, puzzled. "Does it work?"

I smiled. "Well, I doubt it actually works, but you could say a silent prayer as you blow on it. Here." I handed him the stalk topped with a giant ball of fluff. "You know, some prayers are just between us and God."

He held the sticky stalk in his little hand. "It's kinda prickly." He looked up at me with his soft-blue eyes, "What if I want to tell you?"

I knew what he would pray for. "You can tell me, but maybe it's good to practice praying straight to God in your head. He hears everything."

The following week we sat Jake down to tell him we were going to have a baby girl. His eyes lit up. He started to say something, and then refrained and simply smiled.

The King wrapped His new gift, weaving her within her mother's womb.

"This child will be different from your first, My love. I will fashion her to rise and lift My name wherever she goes, carried by the wind of My Spirit. My countenance will be upon her. I will place My fire in her bones, and she will be like the wildflower when it's blown, planting seeds of glory everywhere she goes."

We considered our good fortune and choose the name Jessica, meaning "wealthy." God was blessing us with another great treasure.

Kathy invited me to be there when her son was born, and she was there with Brad and me when our Jessie was born early the following year.

Seeing our family grow, Brad and I considered how much our lives had changed.

Another gift. Thank You, God.

One afternoon I was spending time thanking Father for all He'd done. I quietly sang the song, "I want to care for others like Jesus cares for me."

I'd not finished the song when suddenly I felt the weighty presence of the King. It was as if a barrel of His intoxicating love were poured onto me. I was washed—dowsed—in compassion for Nick.

An overwhelming desire to see him united to Christ flooded me. The hurt and unforgiveness of the past had already been washed away by Christ's grace, but this was a deeper hunger, and I knew the source.

Jesus. He's got to hear about You.

I went to sleep that night praying for Nick and then dreamt about him that night. It was a dream entirely different from the nightmares of my past.

In this dream Nick was dying and needed a blood transfusion. I was the only one with a match for his unique blood type. The hitch was it would take more blood than I could readily, safely share.

The doctor informed me I may or may not live, but for certain Nick would die without it. The physician assured me he'd come in confidence; no one would know if I chose not to go ahead with the transfusion.

The dream was so real and weighty. I made the choice to give my blood. Nick and I were placed in a hospital room together before the transfusion, though we didn't talk. We were put under a heavy sleep. Would I awaken? Would he?

I woke after the transfusion in a room by myself. The doctor appeared and informed me the transfusion was a success. Nick and I would both go on to live healthy lives. The dream ended and I woke.

I'd had good dreams and bad dreams over the years, but none with such clarity and inspiration.

Jesus, what more can I do?

After Brad and I prayed about it, he suggested I go see Nick personally, adding, "I think Kathy should go with you." He would stay with the kids. "Jesus always sent people to minister in pairs, and it makes sense, Shelly." He was right and Kathy agreed.

It had been a while since I sent Nick the letter. Had he even read it? Would he meet with me?

Miss Toni and Dan were no longer married. I'd recently found out that Dan was quite ill. We could stop and see him too.

My heart raced as I dialed Nick's number.

How long has it been? Will I revert to that weak and fearful young girl?

Nick answered. He sounded the same.

Lord help me. I feel like the old Shelly.

"Hi, Nick. It's Shelly." I asked if he'd received my letter. He had. His tone was reserved and understandably apprehensive.

God this is so awkward.

"Go on, child. I am in You. We've got this."

I told Nick I would like to see him. "Dan's very sick, and I'm hoping to see him. I'd really like to see you too. There are some big things that have happened in my life I'd like to share with you. It's all good."

It was a short and awkward conversation, but he agreed to have lunch with me and my friend.

Kathy and I booked flights and made arrangements to stay with a friend of Mom's. We prayed and readied our hearts.

My heart was full of expectation to see what God would do. I was glad Kathy was going with me. She had a disarming way and a quick wit. Everybody loved Kathy. Nick would not be put off by her. If anything, Kathy would put him at ease.

The day arrived to go. Our flight landed in Albuquerque just in time to make our connecting flight to Phoenix. I called Nick to confirm the time and location for lunch the following day. Our next flight was already boarding.

"You know what, Shelly?" He paused. "I've changed my mind."

What? Father? Was Nick really saying this?

Maybe he needed a different time. "We can change the time, if that's an issue." The trip was for him. "Nick, I really want to see you. We're in Albuquerque now."

I saw the other passengers lining up to board.

Nick's voice was tight. "No. I don't think so. I don't want to see you."

I was stumped. I had considered a number of reactions, including a rejection of Jesus, but I didn't expect not to see Nick.

The announcement came over the loudspeaker. "Flight 515 to Phoenix, section C now boarding." It was time. Kathy was beside me, getting the gist of the conversation. Her head was bowed in silent prayer.

"Okay, Nick. Give me just three minutes. We're about to board. Please hear me out. I won't bother you further." Another pause, but he didn't hang up.

"Shelly, just say whatever it is you have to say."

I remembered the verse in Matthew where Jesus promised that God would supply words as we needed them. I did a mental stat prayer and opened my mouth. I didn't think about the words; they simply spilled out: words of hope, care, forgiveness, salvation, purpose.

I finished with a commitment. "Nick, I'm not trying to get into your life, but I want you to know I care about you and where you spend the rest of eternity. God's got a place for you, but you have to say yes, and Jesus is the only way."

I only had seconds left. "I have been praying for you and will continue to pray every day. Nick, I want to see you in heaven."

That was it. "Okay, Shelly. Thanks." He said goodbye. Click and dial tone.

We boarded the plane stunned. We'd bought tickets so we could personally deliver the message. We sat in silence for several minutes. Kathy held my hand. She understood and shared my disappointment.

Wow, God. This wasn't what I expected.

I could sense His presence as we sat there baffled. The plane took off and the wheels left the ground.

Lord. I don't understand.

I'd often heard people say that when God calls us to an assignment, it may not necessarily make sense. Well, this definitely didn't make sense!

I looked at Kathy, thanking Jesus that she was with me. Nick wasn't ready to receive my message. That was okay. It wasn't about me. It was about obedience and planting good seed. Just like the seed Chip had planted years ago for me, good seed could take time. It was enough just to be walking in forgiveness with a vision of hope.

While we were there we got the opportunity to meet with Dan. Dan was a man's man. He was a tower of a man, with the deepest voice I'd ever heard. I'd known Dan since I was eight. He was a little intimidating, but I liked him. He'd always been tough and gritty.

"Jesus talk" was not a conversation Dan would customarily entertain, at least not with "little Shelly."

Dan was in a losing battle with cancer—and in his dying days. It was strange to see this mighty man in such a lowly state. He was lying in bed, a mere shell of the man I remembered. Of course, he made every effort to sound like the same old Dan I knew. "Hey there. It's little Shelly. Whattaya know, kid?"

We made small talk, but I was a little taken aback. Kathy stepped in with her "knows no stranger" manner. She engaged Dan and had him talking as if they'd known each other all along. By the end of our hour, Kathy had graciously, comfortably steered the conversation to ask Dan what he knew about where he was ultimately going. We discussed sin. We talked about Jesus as the only way to get heaven. Dan said he knew about Jesus, "and Lord knows I'm a sinner, but I know where I'm going." Kathy prayed with him a prayer of repentance. Dan knew that he had an entry ticket to heaven.

We said goodbye and I snatched one more glance, exchanging a quiet smile with Dan.

"Thanks for coming, little Shelly."

As Kathy and I drove back to get our bags and make our way to the airport, we both understood why we were there. God always sees more than we do. We were humbled at the privilege to have been there.

Lord.

There was nothing I could say.

"Yes, child. I know My plans and reveal them as I choose to. I will adorn you with grace as you choose to place your feet on My path. Wisdom and humility will be the light by which you see where to place your steps.

"This is how you love Me."

The Great King stood once again among the beautiful banquet tables. He placed another stone on the crisp white linen.

11

NEW HEIGHTS

*W*hen you are sick, the smell of food can push you into dry heaves. But once you become well, you regain an appetite. As you begin to eat, you realize you are famished. You have to replenish your body with nourishment and substance.

Brad and I were no longer sick, but we were ravenous. We'd been spiritually dead so long that when we woke up to *living*, we had a constant appetite and hunger for more. We consumed the Word, followed the King, and looked for more. Could there be more of Jesus?

James, a friend from our small group, began talking about the power of God. James had suddenly become full of life and confidence. He had joy and peace that weren't as evident before. He couldn't stop talking about what God was doing in his life. It wasn't obnoxious but intriguing. He would share things from the Bible that the rest of us were missing. He seemed to have . . . more.

When we asked James what was going on, he just gave an enormous smile and with eyes lit up, he said, "It's the Holy Spirit." James spoke about the Holy Spirit as if He were a person, not some ethereal vapor without will or personality. We were intrigued and wanted to know more.

As a child, I was taught there are three parts to God: Father, Son, and Holy Ghost. The whole "Holy Ghost" thing was kind of weird. I didn't understand it but hadn't needed to.

We didn't have God *wrong*; but if there was more, we wanted more.

God, I want to know all about You. I want as much of You as I can have.

James went on, talking about power and gifts and spiritual authority.

We'd never heard about this. It was strange but exciting.

God, You have done so much. What more is there than having life eternal and experiencing You this side of heaven?

We went to the church leaders with a burning question: "So when are you going to tell us about the Holy Spirit and power and gifts?" They had shown us the love of Christ, and we couldn't wait to hear more. We didn't get the answers we hoped for.

"Oh, that was for the days of the disciples. It doesn't apply now."

But we had seen it in James. And we had read Jesus' promise in Acts 1:8: "But you will receive power when the Holy Spirit has come upon you; and you shall be My witnesses both in Jerusalem, and in all Judea and Samaria, and even to the remotest part of the earth." So, we asked God about it.

We're Your disciples, too, Jesus. Don't we need it as much as they did back then? If there's more, show us in Your Word. Teach us.

We had also read, "You do not have because you do not ask" (James 4:2). We checked our motives and kept on asking. Either our friend was flaking out and full of nonsense, or there really was more.

We dug deeper into our Bibles, searching everything we could on the Holy Spirit. He had pursued us so faithfully; now we were pursuing Him. The more we searched, the more we found.

There *is* more. There is power.

It became apparent that the power is all about being equipped for God's purposes—to reach the hearts of men with the compassion of Christ in powerful ways.

Brad was cutting the lawn one day and correlated the lawn mower with God's power. "Why would you cut grass with scissors when you can use a lawn mower?"

In the book of Matthew we read, "Ask, and it will be given to you; seek, and you will find; knock, and it will be opened to you. For everyone who asks receives, and he who seeks finds, and to him who knocks it will be opened" (7:7–8). We asked. Jesus opened the door, and we met the Holy Spirit, the same Spirit promised in the book of John: "He [the Father] will give you another Helper that He may be with you forever; that is the Spirit of truth, whom the world cannot receive, because it does not see Him or know Him, but you know Him because He abides with you and will be in you" (14:16–17).

As the Holy Spirit revealed the gifts and tools available to us, we realized He was not a strange part of God. In fact, we already knew Him; we just hadn't acknowledged Him.

The more we asked and sought, the more He revealed Father's incredible gifts, weapons for warfare and power tools to advance the kingdom. I had the sense of Father's presence excitedly watching over His children, waiting for us to open another gift. I remembered Nick's excitement as we opened gifts at Christmas.

God, this is so cool.

It was outright fun. God is majestic, high, and holy, worthy of praise and reverence; but there we were, having fun as we drew closer to the Most High God.

We wanted to be in a place where we could learn more about the kingdom of God; so we set out looking for a community of believers who embraced the full Word of God: the teachings of Jesus *and* the power and presence of His Holy Spirit.

Our family, Kathy and her family, James, and a couple of other friends ventured together in search of a place to connect and grow balanced in the disciplines of faith and the power of God.

It was interesting to see the different mixes and beliefs of the church. Some churches would have nothing to do with the Holy Spirit, and others were so focused on the power of the Spirit that they neglected the compassion and kindness of reaching people at their point of need.

Honestly, some churches were just outright strange. The strange ones seemed to be so heavenly minded they served no earthly good. They reminded me of those I'd encountered on my earlier spiritual ventures, which seemed void of Christ. There was a focus on self rather than on honoring the King or serving others in need.

We knew we were home when we visited a small church that welcomed us with warmth and authenticity. They displayed both the kindness of Christ and a hunger for more. Pastor Steve and Lisa welcomed all with open arms. When the service started and the music began, I saw a few hands rise toward the sky. It wasn't showy or in your face; people simply wanted to lift their hands in praise to the unseen King. My heart raced with excitement.

After all we had been through, it had been difficult not to lift my hands, singing to Father. I wanted to raise my voice and my arms and shout from the rooftops, "Do you know what He's done?"

This was home.

As we purposed to learn more of God, His power, and His gifts, we found Him wanting more of us. He continued to clean us from the inside out.

While we sought more, I became aware of a stirring within me. There was something unsettled—an edginess.

Father, what's going on?

It was as if I could go no further. I didn't see Him as I had that first day of fully recognizing Him, but I knew He heard my prayers. I heard His kind words of peace.

"Follow Me."

Still, I didn't understand the inner conflict rising in me.

Jesus, I want more. What's holding me back?

I had the distinct impression that I should talk with our friend James. The next time Brad invited James over for dinner, we sat down and I shared what was going on. I laid everything on the table, including all of the spiritual things I had pursued before surrendering to Jesus. I exposed all the stuff that now seemed very dark to me. I talked about how I'd explored a host of different venues, trying to find answers and satisfaction in the years of hating God, from tea leaves to palm reading, from seeking a higher power to dabbling with inner child exercises. I had even entertained a fascination with numerology and had played with a friend's Ouija board.

I had a new and growing sense that there could be some generational ties to the occult through my family lineage in Freemasonry. As I talked about all these dark endeavors, I realized there had been much more than I recognized. I had never given a second thought to any of it until I sought more of God's Spirit.

What I shared was history. I had let go of all those things when I clasped the hand of Christ two years earlier. It wasn't part of who I was now. I wasn't practicing or engaging in those things any longer, and I had no desire to do so.

What did it matter?

Still, it felt as if I were somehow connected to the dark practices, and I told James as much. Even as I did, I considered the whole thing rather surreal.

Okay; this is weird, Jesus.

"James, I don't know why I should be telling you these things, but I believe the Lord encouraged me to share this with you. What does it have to do with me wanting more of Jesus?"

James was nonplussed. "Shelly, I believe the Lord invited you to share these things with me because I am going to tell you it sounds to me like you are being oppressed by darkness."

I was shocked and offended by his response. "What? James, you know what Father has done in my life, in my marriage. I'm not the same as I used to be."

I had a relationship with Father. He had placed His heart in me. I would not discredit all He had done.

I was more mad than hurt. "James, what do you mean?"

James, unmoved by my exasperation, explained. "I know all that, Shelly. I'm not disregarding what God has done, but what you've described are grounds for demonic influences."

Darkness. Demonic influence? Jesus, what is he talking about?

"That's all history, James. How can I have the King in my heart and have a demonic influence in my life at the same time? The two cannot be in the same place." I looked at him, expecting him to apologize for the bad joke. It was uncharacteristic for him, and I didn't think it was funny.

But James wasn't joking. He went on. "Shelly, you shared this with me and asked why I think the Lord would have you do so. It sounds to me like He wants to do more housecleaning so He can have greater occupancy in you."

It was awkward concluding the conversation. "James, I'm gonna have to search this out between Him and me."

James agreed. "That's what He wants, isn't it?"

As much as we loved and trusted our friend, I needed to get the truth straight from the Lord. So, I went to the Word. I scoured the Old and New Testaments and prayed.

I found more about the unseen spirit realm as I searched the Scriptures. There's a whole world existing beyond our sight that affects our lives. The Bible talks about it. Jesus talked about it. I understood we are hosts for God's presence. After all, the Bible says, "Do you not know that you are a temple of God and that the Spirit of God dwells in you?" (1 Corinthians 3:16).

I hadn't considered that darkness would try to oppress me. This blew me away.

Maybe there are dark influences, obstacles in my walk.

All this took place when we began attending the Harvest. We were only there a few weeks when Pastor Steve welcomed a guest leader, Bruce Shimwell, a pastor from South Africa. Pastor Shimwell was a tall, distinguished, older gentleman. He was soft-spoken, but he walked in the knowledge, authority, and understanding of Jesus. There was a strong presence about him of peace, kindness, humility, and authority—the likes of which I had not seen in any man before.

He gave a message on how the Lord cares about us in the big and small details of our lives. He concluded the message, applying it to the people right there in the room. He was a total stranger directly identifying personal details of individuals to let them know God cared about them.

The whole church consisted of only about forty or fifty people. My mom had come to town and joined us for the service. After addressing Kathy's husband, Pastor Shimwell turned to Mom and spoke things about her no one else would know. He was accurate, detailed, encouraging, and direct. Everything he said pointed to Christ.

He had knowledge he could not have on his own. After addressing a few more people with these special words of encouragement, he asked if anyone needed healing.

Kathy's Mom, Olimay, raised her hand. She was due for another back surgery and had limited range of motion. She was also plagued with grand mal seizures from epilepsy. She'd had more than four hundred major seizures and was on heavy medications.

Olimay stood beside Pastor Shimwell so he could pray for her. As he prayed, Olimay's leg came forward and her spine adjusted before our very eyes.

Later, Pastor Shimwell prayed further with her, and she was healed from the seizures. (She subsequently returned to her physician, who tested her and was baffled by the unexplainable results. She went off her medications entirely and had no further seizures.)

Meanwhile, I stood at the back of the sanctuary, holding a crying baby, Jessie. I watched the man and recognized he was one who knew and understood the authority of Christ.

Now I was convinced. There was, in fact, much more, and I wanted it! I wanted more of Jesus. If that meant there were additional areas to be cleaned and cleared, bring it.

I was ready to deal with it.

Lord, surely if he looks at me, he'll see what I've been battling. Let him call me out. I don't care what people think. I want to be free for more of YOU.

Pastor Shimwell didn't call on me, and eventually the room cleared, as hours had passed in the excitement. It was Memorial Day weekend, and a picnic was to follow the service. It was already three o'clock—well past the lunch hour.

Pastor Shimwell had been speaking and ministering for at least five hours. I knew he was ready to rest.

But I was desperate. I had to approach him.

Lord, give me boldness; I need help.

I went up to Pastor Shimwell while holding a now-exhausted, sleeping Jessie against my shoulder. I briefly explained my inner battle and recent findings.

"I know it's late, but I see that you understand the authority of Christ. I don't know how . . ." I was at a loss for words. I blurted out the most relevant scripture that came to my mind, Matthew 15:27: "'. . . but even the dogs feed on the crumbs which fall from their masters' table.' Can you help me?"

I shifted Jessie in my arms and briefly explained how I'd begun to see there could be a correlation between family connections to Freemasonry and occult practices I had dabbled in.

I didn't know what to do about it though I was not actively

embracing any of it. "I just want more Jesus, but this stuff keeps rising up in my thoughts the more I press in."

His eyes met mine. It was only seconds, but I felt as if he saw every dark thing still in me. He then lowered his head and began praying. He spoke gently but authoritatively, addressing darkness from generational curses.

Looking at Jessie, he asked, "Is this your daughter?" I nodded. He added, "Is there someone who can hold her?"

Mom was at my side. "I'm Shelly's mom. I can take her."

I handed Jessie to Mom. Jessie remained asleep.

Pastor Shimwell gently laid his hand on my head and continued praying. A minute later he looked up, opening his violet-blue eyes and turned to Jessie, though he didn't stop his words.

He lifted my hand. "Put your hand on her and agree with me. In the name of Jesus, I break the generational curse of early death upon this family and generations to come, including this child. It stops here."

I watched Jessie's little body tremble. Her entire body shook as if in a convulsion. Strangely, I was not alarmed. Pastor Shimwell continued, "In its place I speak forth life and longevity and goodness that You, Lord, be magnified."

The trembling stopped with these words. Jessie continued sleeping, undisturbed. Pastor Shimwell finished. "That's it, my dear."

I knew there was more. "There's more."

He simply smiled, tiredly, and said, "There may well be, but call on your pastor and he will walk you through this."

I was stunned. I had a list of things I knew I needed to be cleared of before the Lord, but death?

My grandmother and grandfather had both died young. Two other relatives in prior generations had also died young on my father's side. I had not considered this.

How could he have possibly known?

I shared the news with Brad when I joined up with him later at the church picnic. We looked over to the noisy ball field where Olimay was playing ball with the children and showing everyone how she could bend and touch her toes—an action she had not done in years. Our lives were marked once again by the power of the King that day.

That week I connected with our new pastor, telling him of my exchange with Pastor Shimwell. "He said I should call on you if there was more. He said you could help walk me through this." I trembled inwardly. "Pastor Steve, there is more."

Pastor Steve and another pastor friend, Eric, came to our house two days later to hear my story. They sat and listened as I laid my heart before them. As they listened, I saw kindness and excitement in their eyes. I was relieved.

As I relayed the point of Pastor Shimwell's prayer, Pastor Steve suddenly looked at his watch and frantically apologized. "Shelly, I am so sorry. We have to leave right now. I am supposed to be at a wedding rehearsal at this very moment. We will have to meet another time. Can we resume tomorrow evening?"

I sat stunned again. I knew they'd been there well over an hour, and looking at them, I could see they felt bad. "Of course."

God, what is going on? Why does this continue to get delayed?

I thought of the verse that says, "Surely, as I have planned, so it will be, and as I have purposed, so it will happen," (Isaiah 14:24 NIV) and knew it was His answer to me.

Later that evening, Kathy's crew, James, and a few other friends came over. We spent time in worship and prayer, thanking God for all He was doing.

We prayed for more of Father in us. I had asked for the gift of tongues weeks before, but with so much darkness stirring in me, I thought it better to pray for others instead of myself.

Lord, what gift do You have for Brad?

As I silently prayed, asking more for Brad and my friends, I had a sense that if I opened my own mouth, strange words would come out of me.

Jesus? Is this the gift of tongues? For me?

I was excited but hesitated. Logic and reasoning raced through my mind.

You really are going out on the deep end now.

This is nonsense.

That psychiatrist was right: you've got issues.

You're crazy.

I took a deep breath and harnessed my thoughts.

Jesus!

Then I considered that, if there was a demonic presence, maybe I could unknowingly be speaking curses if I gave voice to the strange language welling up in me. It was ignorance, but I wanted to be careful. I would wait till everyone left for the night.

Usually when Kathy and her crew were over, the evening ended sooner than I liked. It was always a rich time of fellowship and opportunity to dig into God's Word. Tonight, though, I was excited when everyone left. There was a sort of fluttering rising from deep within. I pictured a bright, gentle bubbling like the liquid gold of Christ's presence I'd perceived in the last two years.

We said goodbyes, closed the door, and I hurried to get alone in a closet. I eagerly wanted to open my mouth and release to Father the words of love and adoration that came with the utterances that rose from inside.

As soon as I did, a fresh flood of peace fell upon me. I became acutely aware of the presence of Father. It was personal and intimate.

Joy welled up, and my awareness of the King was strong and vibrant. Father was in control in me. I had nothing to fear with this inner battle. It was real, and Father was simply cleansing me again at a deeper level. He was making room for more.

I embraced the gift and prayed in a new language late into the night. I fell asleep talking to the Lord, adoring His presence.

The next morning a storm rolled in. Heavy gray clouds hung low, unleashing a downpour of rain. Gusts of wind hammered sheets of rain in a horizontal fury. Brad and Jake had scheduled a guys' day, so they left for lunch and a movie.

The storm continued and intensified as bolts of lightning flashed and booms of thunder reverberated.

I sat Jessie in her bouncy seat on the counter while I chopped vegetables for soup. Another clap of thunder followed immediately after the room lit up with light flashing through windows. The house shook.

"Hey, little one, that sure was close wasn't it?" I said to Jessie as she followed me with her eyes. I kissed her tiny pink toes as she bounced.

The storm outside reflected the battle warring inside me. It felt as if fire were in my bones, though I was not afraid. I moved Jessie to the other side of the counter, further from the window. As soon as I set her down, the light directly above where she'd previously been burst. Glass shattered directly onto the spot from which I'd just removed her. I should have been alarmed, but instead, I silently thanked God for protection. Father's surpassing peace continued steady within me.

God, this is wild, but I'm holding on.

I continued with my new gift, lifting my heart to the King.

The lights flickered. Lightning shot bright flashes against the walls, and an ear-piercing crack of electrical turbulence shot through the house. As the storm outside intensified, my insides quivered. Lightning struck a tree in our neighbor's yard just outside the kitchen window. I was aware that Jess was studying my response to the outer storm. She mirrored the calm within as I spoke softly to her. "I love you, little one."

I knew what Jesus was saying to me.

"She needs to learn peace in the midst of chaos. Peace. Teach her peace."

Lord, I know You are here.

The Great Warrior stood over the mother and child, unmoved by the enemy's mediocre scare tactics against the mother.

Protector and enemy both knew the war was won already, but the enemy always relished in poking his prey to the furthest extent. The Protector would allow His child to remain in the storm, knowing His truth and character would grow in her—fortified through the onslaught.

The enemy capitalized on this truth. His nature was to fight and carry each battle out as long as he could. It did not matter if he lost. His goal was to oppose the Protector and defeat His flock. If he could elongate their suffering, he was all the more satisfied.

The Protector flooded the mother with fresh light, dispelling the dark arrows of the enemy aimed at her mind.

"Steady, child. I've already won."

I had a sense—an awareness—that the enemy had one last foothold in me and didn't want to give up that occupied territory. But the clock was ticking for the last strongholds of the enemy to be demolished. Any other time I would have been freaked-out. This was over-the-top —ridiculously strange.

I picked up another carrot, speaking gently to Jessie. "And carrots are good for the soup. Carrots and onions and . . ." Jessie's smile captured my attention. How I loved this little girl before me.

Jesus, I trust You. I know I'm Yours. I know You're here. Take every part that does not belong in Your temple.

The darkness that lay dormant in my heart and mind was stirred up. The hunger for more of Jesus could no longer be bound. The two opposing influences seemed at war. Their presence was almost palpable. Darkness tightened its grip with each step I took toward the gifts of God.

I waited for Brad and Jake as I laid Jess down for a nap. She slept through the remainder of the storm, and eventually both the storm outside of our house and the one inside my heart subsided.

That evening Pastor Steve returned with two elders. We spent time in conversational prayer, talking to and listening to Jesus as the Holy Spirit worked in me like a torch, exposing hidden places in my heart and mind that were closed off from Christ.

I had experienced freedom, but now it was as though invisible chains that restrained me to a limited domain lay broken at my feet. I felt as if a physical weight had lifted off, even out, of me. And I remembered the scripture: "Jesus said, 'The thief comes only to steal and kill and destroy. I came that they may have life and have it abundantly'" (John 10:10).

I experienced the power of God in and through me that night. It was not unlike when I first became aware of His presence. It was more. There was more understanding of the power and authority of Jesus in us over the works of darkness—our unseen opponent.

I began to understand what Jesus spoke of to His first disciples when He foretold of the Holy Spirit in Luke 4:18: "The Spirit of the Lord is upon me, because He has anointed me to preach the gospel to the poor. He has sent me to proclaim release to the captives, and recovery of sight to the blind, to set free those who are oppressed." (Luke 4:18)

He really does entrust His children with His authority and equip us with His power.

Soon after that, we did a study on forgiveness, and I began to see more in everything.

Jesus, You forgive and You lead us to forgive others. What could be more than Your forgiveness? I can't be more forgiven than by You — or can I?

Remember my dirty little secret I carried from California? It was washed away at the cross and removed the moment I released my heart and fully welcomed Jesus' heart in me. I was free from that sin, but it was still a *secret* I protected Brad from. With the secret, there was still a residue of shame.

The more I turned to Jesus in every big and little thing, the more I yearned to have all trace of my dirty secret clear and clean in the full light of grace. It would have been wrong to go to Brad, and say, "Hey, I want to be free from this secret . . ." It was history, and it was a hurtful truth.

Jesus, I know You forgave me. That sin no longer has a hold on me, but it's a hidden sin. I lay it at Your feet and trust You and Your timing. If You want to clear it between Brad and me, please make it very clear and give me grace to speak in such a way so as not to hurt him. Above all let there be peace and oneness between Brad and me.

That was it. I left it alone and kept an open ear to the matter. Maybe Jesus didn't need that to be sifted through Brad's heart.

One day, months later, Brad and I were talking about forgiveness and trust. This was already a sensitive issue because of the journal reading years earlier. I knew that while you can forgive a person, you can also not trust them in certain areas. My heart was pumping hard, and my insides quaked.

Brad asked probing questions.

Oh, Lord, here it is. I'm holding on. Holy Spirit, help me.

We had come so far. I didn't want to backtrack. I asked, "Do you really want to know?" I was tempted to gloss over it, but I had prayed about it.

There's no getting around the fact that it was a hard blow. It was awful. Brad had not suspected specifics, but he had known something had been amiss with the Zoe relationship. "Shelly, I didn't know what, but I knew there was something." Now it was out—no longer a secret between us.

Trusting me, however, was a different issue. What was history for me was, for Brad, a fresh betrayal. He was deeply hurt and needed time to heal. I felt terrible. I knew I would have to earn back his trust.

But Lord, that has no part in our lives now. I have no desire for those dark affections. Can't You take away this awkwardness and speed up the healing?

His reply was caring. "This really hurt him, Shelly. Let him heal. There *are consequences to sin.*"

It was painful for both of us. Brad did forgive me, though it took time to rebuild trust—much more time than I wanted. Love is patient, and I was grateful for more forgiveness.

Through this, Jesus taught me that though He'd already forgiven me—and we can't get any cleaner than by His blood—there is more. I marveled as I began to understand that when the Spirit of God extends forgiveness through imperfect man, whose nature is not to forgive, Christ is magnified over and again.

The King always has MORE.

The Great Teacher looked on as His children grasped His ways—each learning in their own unique fashion. A soft and satisfied smile spread across the chiseled expanse of His noble face. He watched the image of His Son reflected in this son and daughter as they began to walk out His instruction.

LIVING THINGS GROW

*W*e settled into our new norm. It was good and felt right. I was fascinated at how much was changing in us. I'd watch Brad smiling with sheer delight as he watched Jake chasing Jessie.

"I'm . . . gonna . . . GET you and tickle you from your toes to your nose!" Jake would yell, lunging for his sister as she giggled wildly, seeking safety behind Brad's back.

Jesus, we look different, don't we? I believe we really did. The weariness of fighting life had faded. Brad's expression was somehow softer, as if it were lit up with peace and joy.

Soon we were praying over another new life. Jake would take Jessie's hand and place it on my growing tummy. "Jesus, thank You for this little baby. Please make her strong with a big heart."

Jessie was only eighteen months old. I could see the puzzled thoughts in her eyes; how did the baby get in Momma's belly? She turned to study Jake. Obviously convinced it didn't matter, she proudly ended with an emphatic, "Yeah. Uh-huh. Amen!"

I wrapped my arms around them, squeezing tight.

The King understood, pleased at the work of His hands.

"Yes, and this next child will have her own unique spin from Me. I am giving her My hunger to explore and expand and quietly tend deep pain in others. My water will run deep through her. She will shine and reflect Me in different ways than the others. This one will be like a stream, soft and subtle in her approach, but silently carving and shaping new pathways in the desert places. I am pleased to call her Mine as I entrust her to you. Teach these children well, My love, but also watch and learn from them. They are gifts that I share with you—a pillar, a fire, and a stream."

Anna became the signature of our family. God's favor and grace was truly on us. I was amazed God had entrusted us with yet another child, and I loved being a stay-at-home mom.

Kathy was at the hospital when Jessie and Anna were born, and I was there when her boys were born. We did life together. Thanksgiving, birthdays, Saturday nights, play days, and so on. We were either at their house or they were at ours. "Mom, when is Ali coming over?" Jake would often ask, referring to Kathy's oldest daughter.

When Brad and I finally purchased our first home, Kathy was beside me, washing filthy blinds and scrubbing floors. When the girls outgrew their clothes, Kathy was there with bags of hand-me-downs.

I even followed Kathy's lead in trying homeschooling instead of kindergarten. When Kathy decided to take homeschooling past kindergarten, I wanted to do the same—but could I?

Kindergarten was safe and reasonable. It wasn't really homeschooling, I told myself. I could teach Jake shapes, colors, and numbers, but first grade was a little more serious. I approached real homeschooling shaking in my boots.

God, can I do this?

Kathy was a great inspiration, and the curriculum was a lifesaver, but homeschooling was a stretch for me. Second grade was a remedial year, but it was still a challenge.

Lord, what if I mess him up?

As each year increased in complexity, my confidence in teaching decreased. By Jake's third grade year, I struggled to keep on track. I didn't connect my own learning challenges to my difficulty in teaching.

Do I have to log every lesson plan? Ugh. Why do we have to teach sentence structure? I didn't get it the first time around.

Then Jake would do something in our little classroom that would spur me on. I remember reading a paper he wrote on his perception of the days of creation. He described his impression of what Adam and Eve heard when "the man and his wife heard the sound of the Lord God as He was walking in the garden in the cool of the day" (Genesis 3:8 NIV).

Jake wrote, "I think that when they heard God walking in the Garden, it musta sounded like a thousand elephants."

Wow, God.

It was fun to watch Jake learning where I had struggled. He actually understood what I taught. But even as I taught, I had a hard time keeping up with him. By spring of third grade, both Jake and I were counting down the days to summer break.

Jenny called just before we finished the school year.

"Guess what?" she said, and I was excited to hear her voice. I knew she really liked the guy, Mark, she was dating. They sounded serious.

"Shelly," she continued. "I'm engaged!"

"Oh my gosh, Jenny! Engaged? Wow! Congratulations." My little sister was getting married. I laughed with her. "That is awesome, Jen!"

"Yeah, I'll be sure and email you engagement pictures." She paused and we both took a second reflecting how her life was about to change. "Shelly, I'm getting married!"

I flew out for the engagement party and met Mark. He was warm, engaging, and funny. I really liked him, and it was a thrill to see Jenny so happy. My baby sister was now a young woman.

Dad, Miss Ellie, and Chris were at the party. I hoped to catch a quick, more personal visit with them later before I left back for Dallas.

Dad invited me to come to their property outside of town. He was building his own house. "Not much to see just yet, but you're welcome to come take a peek." He smiled his quirky way, raising one eyebrow, "I just finished laying the foundation."

Of course I would go!

Jenny let me borrow her car. Dad's property was just under a two-hour drive from Jen's place. On the drive there I considered what a big deal this was for Dad. He'd designed the house himself, and now he was building it. As a child I had heard Dad talk about his dream to build a house on a mountain. He talked about it for years. In fact, as a family we used to drive the desert foothills looking for the perfect spot.

My insides stirred when I arrived and saw his dream emerging on the foundation he'd just completed. The giant slab was strong, smooth, and solid. It lay upon a beautiful piece of land at the top of a small mountain, overlooking a train track and a dry riverbed. The views were fantastic in each direction.

And there was my dad, walking toward me in his Levi grunges, hat, and gloves. He was laying the cornerstones with his own hands.

He gave me the visionary tour. "This is where the kitchen will be and the dining room. See this tree? Over here we'll have a large patio extending to the garden." He would later name it Castle of the Blue Garden for the raw cobalt stones he lined along the garden pathway.

I was so proud to see Dad building his dream with brick and mortar using his mind, body, and heart. Dad was building his house, and so was Father. My heart overflowed with gratitude, and I prayed with heartfelt joy, "Thank you, God, for bringing me to this place and time!"

The Great I AM admired the curves of the smooth stone gate leading from heaven's banquet hall to the garden path. The sound of the children's laughter mingled with the babbling brook.

Sound, scent, and sight were clear, clean, and vibrant on heaven's side of the great veil. Earth's side was beautiful, but to walk on earth was to perceive as an unborn child perceives within the womb: seeing, tasting, feeling and hearing—but only in part.

Drawing near to the garden's center, the King looked upon the ancient Tree of Life. Succulent fruit hung full among its mighty branches. When the Great Feast commenced, the fruit would be the delight of all. Life eternal.

It had grieved Him deeply the day He'd had to cast His children away from that beautiful tree and out of the sacred garden lest they eat of the fruit and live forever in their sin. His Son had stepped out of the garden and into humanity to make a bridge back. It was good to have Him home. Now they were preparing for the feast and the great assembly. The Holy Spirit and the angels were tending to the earth.

It wouldn't be long.

Summer ended and the "Busby school" started back up. Later that fall, we took a break for Jenny's wedding.

This would be the first time Mom and Dad would be in the same place since my wedding. So much had happened since then. The family dynamics had changed. Mom had divorced Nick. Ben was now married. Jenny was getting married. Christine was in Spain for school. Brad and I were different too. We had three kids and a life centered around Christ. Considering all the changes, I wondered—*how will this play out?*

This also would be our first real trip with all three kids. They were ecstatic. "We get to go on a plane!"

We woke at 3:30 a.m. to get to the airport on time. The first flight was fun. The girls chased each other at the terminal as we waited for our connecting flight in Albuquerque. The second flight was not so fun.

"No fair. Jake gets the good seat."

"I'm bored."

"I'm out of snacks."

"I have to go potty."

By the time we got to our hotel, it was 3 p.m., and the girls were exhausted.

I called Dad to see if we could see them before the reception dinner the next night. There would be a crowd, and I wanted some special time with him and Miss Ellie.

"Yeah, kid. Miss Ellie and I would love for you to bring the family out to see the new place. Why don't y'all come out for lunch tomorrow?"

That's when I panicked.

The entire next day was full with bridal party events. The day after was the wedding. The following morning we would be on a flight home.

There was simply no time for the long drive to Dad's and back between all the festivities.

As I contemplated options, I watched a fight brewing between the girls. Anna lay on the side of the bed Jessie had laid claim to with her stuffed bear and suitcase. Jessie was balling up a fist. "That's *my* side!"

"Girls!" I shouted at them, then turned back to the phone. "Sorry, Dad."

We'd come so far literally and figuratively. I was not about to lose the relational territory that had been restored.

Lord, You've got this, right?

I blurted, "Dad, what if we come today?"

It was a ludicrous idea. Dad's place was almost two hours away. And Mark's mom had a special pre-rehearsal dinner planned that night for everyone in from out of town. Not to mention that Mark and Jenny had bought our plane tickets to come for their event.

But it was the only time we could do it. Brad was listening to the conversation. He looked at me like I was crazy as he broke up the girls' escalating fight. We needed to get them something to eat, and they really needed to nap. As ring bearer, Jake still needed to get dropped off with Mark for last-minute tux alterations.

I needed help figuring this out, and silently prayed: *Jesus, help. I could really mess up here. Dad and Miss Ellie will understand if we don't come, but this is important. We won't get this day back for a do-over. Lord? What do You want us to do?*

I was proud of Dad's accomplishment and touched that he and Miss Ellie wanted us all to come see it. This was about more than the house.

"Dad, can I call you right back?" I got off the phone and looked at Brad. "What do we do?" I asked.

He knew the dynamics. "Shelly, what do you want to do?"

"I want to see my Dad and Miss Ellie." This was Dad's castle, built by the "king" himself. "But what about Jenny . . . ?" My thoughts trailed, not wanting to slight anyone.

Brad stopped me and picked up Anna. "We'll drive through a Wendy's. Hopefully, the girls will sleep in the car, and we can make it back for dessert tonight. Call Mark and see if he can pick up Jake. Jenny will understand." I looked at him, a little baffled, and then grabbed my purse and phone. I called Dad back; we loaded up and headed out.

Miss Ellie welcomed us with tender hugs. Her eyes reflected her words, "I'm so glad you guys made it out here." She paused a moment looking us over, picking up on our slightly ragged state. "That's a long drive, especially after flying."

It was obvious it mattered to them that we came. Miss Ellie doted on the girls while Dad gave us the tour. It was just as he had described months earlier. The Castillo del Jardin Azul was all but complete with walls and roof, doors and windows. It was beautiful—a masterpiece, really. A few heavy, blue stones marked the transition from home to desert garden. I took in a deep breath of fresh air as my eyes surveyed the untouched land of rolling hills across the dry riverbed. "Dad this is fantastic. You thought of everything." It was regal but not pretentious.

"You should make a trip out here and spend time with us," Miss Ellie said as she came around the corner holding Jessie's hand. "You know there's plenty of room, and we'd love for you all to come."

I looked at Brad and smiled. "Thanks. We'll see what we can do."

We were at Dad's less than an hour, but it was worth it. The girls crashed in their car seats as we headed back to the valley of the sun.

Yeah, it was a four-hour-plus detour, but I wouldn't trade those forty-eight minutes together for anything. We saw the dream Dad built. I don't regret the time and risk it took. This was one more building block in our relationship.

The next day, Dad walked Jenny down the aisle. Jake was the ring bearer, and Jessie was the flower girl who decided to sit down on the job because her legs were sleepy. I tried to focus, stifling a laugh. Anna had set off the hotel fire alarm earlier. Now she had taken off to chase ducks at a nearby brook, diverting Jessie's attention from flower girl post.

Did You see that, Lord? Ah yes, she's mine!

Jessie left the wedding party and joined Anna, chasing ducks. *And she's mine and he's mine and . . . this is family. We belong to You.*

I thought of the verse in 1 John that says, "Beloved, let us love one another, for love is from God; and everyone who loves is born of God and knows God" (4:7). I knew this was true—God was making it true in our lives!

The sounds of many voices singing, praying, crying out His name rose in the crystal sky. The King savored the sounds. The voices brought Him delight.

All the while He did not lose notice of those strained melodies offered from the dark and lonely places of pain, betrayal, loss, and devastation. Those were always the ones that stirred Him most deeply.

We hit the books when we arrived back in Dallas. As the weeks continued, I struggled more to keep up with the teaching, the curriculum, and the girls. I was in over my head.

This had been going on the last year, but I pressed on every time I thought about Kathy.

She has five kids and does parties and field trips and crafts and she cooks meals from scratch. And . . .

I couldn't keep up the pace.

Lord, help! I love having the kids close with me here. I love our time, but I'm overwhelmed!

One morning Jake and I were in the schoolroom, working on math. We were going round and round about writing out long division. He could do it in his head. He huffed and pounded his fists on the table. "Why do I have to write it out if I know how it works?"

It was long division with long numbers. He could figure in his head, but I couldn't. And because I couldn't track with him I insisted he write it out. In exasperation, I yelled at him and threw a pencil across the room. "I'm the teacher, and this is how we're going to do it! I don't care how smart you are."

Ugh. There it was again . . . the ugliness of me.

Lord, did I really just do and say that?

I sat down beside Jake. "Wow, buddy. I really messed up. That was wrong, and I am so sorry."

He looked at me, obviously hurt. "That's okay, Mom."

"No, Jake, it's really not. You are smart, and I'm proud of you. I got frustrated with myself and took it out on you." Then I whispered, "And I did it in a way one of your sisters would get in trouble for!"

He looked at me sheepishly. "I know."

"Will you forgive me, Jake?"

He gave me a hug, "Yeah, Mom. I forgive you."

The scene was crushing enough, but the reality was there before us. We had taken homeschooling to our furthest extent. Jake deserved better. We met the principal of the school at the end of our street. Jake would begin public school the following month, after winter break.

It was difficult to see Jake off to school each day. I looked in his eyes and saw a little boy wanting to do the right thing. "You're gonna do *great* today, Jake," I said to him on that first day. "I know it's scary, but Dad and I are really proud of you."

He worked up a smile. "Yeah, okay. Thanks, Mom."

It's difficult for a child to enter a new school, but here was this boy entering school for the first time in fourth grade. My stomach was in knots. I prayed, "Oh, God, how I love this boy! Be his confidence and favor. Make up for my lack."

Jake made the adjustments and transitioned well. It took me much longer to adjust to letting go and not feeling that I'd failed.

Soon Jessie was asking when *she* could go to school too. Jessie thrived in the company of many. Our social buzzing bee couldn't wait to get into a classroom full of kids. Jessie was elated when we signed her up for Mothers' Day Out. I missed her presence and couldn't wait to see her bright eyes and bouncing curls when it was time to pick her up.

For the next two years, Anna and I had special time running errands and tending the home together. We'd eagerly go pick up Jessie. Anna's curly-top head would stretch forward as she held my hand, looking for her sister in the crowd.

Later in the day, the girls would excitedly run to welcome Jake home with shouts and hugs. They'd repeat the scene later when Brad came home.

When Anna's turn came to spread her wings, I enrolled her in Mothers' Day Out. It stung even more than the others. There were no more little hands to hold as I went about my daily business. I would miss her belly laughs and quirky ways.

One day I prayed, "Jesus, I don't want this season to end. Will I remember the smell of my little girl's watermelon shampoo or the mornings spent sitting with my little ones as they eat 'moatmeal'? Jake already wants to spend time with friends instead of coming home . . ."

It was as if I could hear him say, "Daughter, you need to let go so you can grasp what lies ahead."

And then He lovingly reminded me of the *fffttt, fffttt, fffttt* sound of Jake's Spidey-Man shoes.

I thought of my own mom. Our relationship had changed entirely. I called her often. "Mom, today Jessie made a goal at soccer!" I wanted to share the special moments. "Mom, Anna found a turtle in the pool. She named it 'Watery' and took it to Mothers' Day Out. You should have seen how proud she was."

Mom had become a friend, and Brad encouraged me to send her a key to the house. I wrapped one in a note and sent it. "If you moved to Dallas, you could come by anytime. No need to knock. Here's the key."

She took it to heart. "You know, Shelly, I just might."

The following year she relocated to Dallas.

It was good to have Mom in our lives. She worked but always made time to spend with family.

"Mom, Jake has an orchestra presentation."

"Shelly, can the girls spend the night?"

"Shelly, I want to take the girls to the Ice Capades."

We would look back on these days without regrets.

Lord, now what?

Jake was in school, and the girls were in kindergarten and Mothers' Day Out. There were toys scattered on the floor and remnants of breakfast on the table, crayon pictures and tempura paintings on the walls. I bent down to pick up muddy shoes and jackets strewn over the couch when it hit me . . .

I was alone for the first time in years.

An empty groan began deep in my stomach. I dropped to my knees, holding Anna's jacket. I pulled it to my face, enjoying the faint smell of her as tears threatened to spill. The familiar voice of Jesus rushed upon me.

"Child, you're not alone. Come on. This is our time."

I looked at the clock and rose back to my feet with new appreciation. I'd almost missed it—special time to be alone with the King before the other blessings in my life returned for the day.

It was a short season, but it was rich. I danced and spun and sang in the quiet hours alone with the Master. Whether quietly lying before Him in prayer or dancing wildly unto Him in the empty house with worship music blaring, those days were full of His presence. I knew it wouldn't last long.

I prayed, "What next, Lord?"

Immediately I thought of the verse in Proverbs: "Trust in the LORD with all your heart, and do not lean on your own understanding. In all your ways acknowledge Him, and He will make your paths straight" (3:5–6)

Shortly after that, I got the phone call. Our little church was growing, and they needed part-time help. Ms. Donna said, "Would you be interested in work as a receptionist?"

I hesitated. I didn't want to lose time with my family.

Donna reassured me, "It's part-time, and you could work when your girls are at school."

We already spent a lot of time at the church; it seemed the natural thing to do. I took the position.

You really get to know people when you work with them—far more than you do in a few minutes' exchange on Sundays. The staff became my family. I grew to love and appreciate them at a deeper level, each with their unique differences.

Pastor Steve was full of wisdom and passion for Jesus, his family, and the flock. He was a friend and a brother. I found in him a strong warrior and worshipper, with a heart like King David's.

Pastor was also like a big kid with ornery, older-brother ways. He taught me much about grace and reminded me not to take myself so seriously. He's the only one I know who could hit you with a two-by-four of solid truth and send you off as you thanked him.

The first time we met Lisa, Pastor Steve's wife, she walked right up to Brad and me and generously welcomed us as if she'd been looking for us for a long time. For all her beauty, she was warm and disarming. Lisa earnestly cared about the flock, always looking beyond the Sunday faces to the heart of individuals. She had the gift of encouragement and would turn every situation back to Jesus. "I wonder what God's going to do with that. You know it's going to be good."

I can still hear her sweet Southern drawl saying, "God knows the plans He has for you."

"Momma" Donna was the backbone of our staff, keeping us in check, on task, and on time. She was passionate about God's Word and—just as Paul exhorted Timothy—she stirred in me a desire to be "diligent to present yourself approved to God as a workman who does not need to be ashamed, accurately handling the word of truth" (2 Timothy 2:15).

She was tough too. I still encounter situations where I can hear Donna ducking her head and whispering, "It's time to put your big-girl panties on," or "Here's a tissue for your issue," or "I don't have time for nonsense." I took to heart her advice that "90 percent of life is just showing up."

For all of Donna's seemingly brash ways, she had a heart of gold. She would go out of her way to help others in practical ways. If Pastor Steve was my big brother, Momma Donna was everyone's big sister. She looked out for everyone.

Later, another Donna came into my life and became a dear close friend. Donna P. was steadfast and kind, a constant encouragement despite the highs and lows of ministry. To me, this woman epitomized Philippians 4:5, which instructs us to "let your gentle spirit be known to all men. The Lord is near."

These were more than friends—they were my people; God's people, always about kingdom business.

Through them, God nurtured us, pruned us, and spurred us on. We learned how to live and love well. Here, we raised our kids in the ways of the King.

As our church grew and our family matured, so did my role on staff. God was using what He'd done in my life to share it forward with others.

We worked for Sundays and Wednesdays—game days. The goal was always to meet people at their point of need with the love of Christ. I loved to talk to Jesus about the changes He was making in lives all around me:

"Jesus, there's another daughter reaching out for You. See how her countenance has changed?"

"Father, that marriage was doomed, but You totally turned it around."

"Lord, see how they love You!"

For all my desire to travel the world, I was happy to be there, serving Father with our people. Whenever I stopped and thought about it, I felt sheer amazement and gratitude! How I loved my life! My history was no longer a shameful secret but a powerful tool to be used to reach others. In fact, it was being used to defeat the enemy's grip in the lives of others.

This verse suddenly took on whole new meaning for me: "And they overcame him [the devil] because of the blood of the Lamb and because of the word of their testimony, and they did not love their life even when faced with death" (Revelation 12:11).

As fulfilling as it was to serve on staff, it was also a challenge. Sometimes you just have to get in the mud with people to meet them at their point of need to show them the way out. You can't slog through a mud bog without getting dirty. I wanted to cry with each aching heart. It was tough to leave the office each afternoon and leave behind the burdens of others so I could be present for my family.

What was even harder was to see people turn away from the face of God and harden their hearts in willful defiance to Him. I knew the signs because for many years I'd been that person. Now it broke my heart to watch when others made the same mistake.

I knew the direction they were headed. I wanted to chase them down, tackle them, get in their face, and yell, *"Stop! Don't do this. It will cost you more than you know, more than you have."*

I had little tolerance for people who wanted the cure but weren't willing to let go of the sin that crippled them. You either reach for Christ with empty hands, or you refuse to put down the very things that are hurting you. Either way, you hold on to what you really want.

Some people chose to walk away with an attitude, if not the actual words that "It's just too difficult. I'm gonna do this my way." My insides would tremble, and my heart would ache.

Jesus, they're being deceived.

I grieved knowing that Father grieved more. I could imagine His words to me: *"Shelly, it's not your battle. It's Mine."*

Slowly, I grew. And the church grew. Eventually our team doubled, then multiplied. The prayers and dreams Father planted in the early years were being answered before our very eyes.

It says in Ecclesiastes 3:1 that "there is an appointed time for everything. And there is a time for every event under heaven." We were watching His appointed timing unfold in the ministry before us.

Little did I know I was about to see His appointed timing at work in my personal relationships as well.

One afternoon Mom called and asked if I could come over. She had news she wanted to share in person.

"Sure," I told her. "I can drop by after work."

Mom was making chili when I walked in. She stirred in the veggies before we sat down to chat.

"I talked with Nick last night," she said, and I could see she was studying my face, looking for a reaction. I looked at her blankly. She folded her hands and took a deep breath. "He wanted me to pass on a message to Ben, Jenny, and you."

I braced myself. We'd been hearing from family friends that Nick's erratic behavior had grown worse over the last several years. Mom had not spoken with him in years until recently, when he had called her multiple times during meltdowns.

During those calls, Nick said crazy things like he suspected he was being watched and followed. He claimed to have amassed a small secret fortune. He also made flippant threats, telling Mom she'd be in danger if she crossed him. Mom told me about those conversations as a precaution. This was nothing new. So what did he want to share?

I had grown to care deeply for Nick through the years of talking to God about him. I knew he was still potentially dangerous, and, in fact, he sounded worse than ever. Even so, he mattered. I longed for His eternal well-being.

My mind had wandered, but Mom got my attention again. "Shelly, Nick asked me to let all three of you kids know that he is very sorry for the things he did over the years. He didn't make excuses. In fact, he acknowledged that he did some very bad things. He wishes he could take it all back."

Mom sat quietly, waiting for me to respond. I was stunned.

Jesus? Has he really owned his sin?

I pondered the possibility.

Wait. Do I believe this? Is this for real? Or is it more of Nick's smack talk?

Mom went on. "Nick wanted you to know that he knows you were praying for him . . . said he never forgot whatever it was you shared with him when you went out to see him."

She paused. My heart lifted with hope. She carefully dispensed her next words as if they were liquid gold. "He said to let you know that He knows what Jesus did for him and he has Him in his heart."

"What?" I rose out of my seat, processing what she'd just said. "Mom, was he—you know—in his right mind?"

"He goes back and forth a lot now, but as he talked about Jesus, he was exceptionally clear and unusually peaceful."

Is this for real, Lord?

Mom waited a minute while I processed the news. I could see there was more.

"Nick's sick, Shelly. He's been diagnosed as bipolar. They think he also struggles with schizophrenia. He was in the hospital for a while, but he's out now. Says he doesn't like taking the medicine; makes him feel like he's sleepwalking. He had to turn in his driver's license."

"What?" But even as I said it, all those years of craziness became instantly clear in that one moment. "Wow." I looked at Mom as we both considered all the years of chaos and suffering. "Wow." I said again. "That totally makes sense, doesn't it?"

She nodded. "He's alone again, and no one wants to deal with him." His third wife, Gwen, had separated from him. "He's just too unstable."

Mom looked out the sliding glass door. It was a clear, blue sky day. "His body is wearing out and he's become more contentious. Pam has stepped back into his life though."

Pam was one of Nick's daughters. Mom continued, "Nick said she's been a tremendous help . . . called her his angel."

I could see this was a lot for Mom to process as well. I sat back down. "So, did it really sound like he had peace? Like he was shooting straight about Jesus? Or do you think it was part of his condition?"

Mom paused. I could see her replaying the conversation with Nick in her mind. Slowly she looked up, her eyes meeting mine. "No, Shelly, I could tell. He was broken. It was important to him that you know."

This news was a bittersweet gift. Bitter to hear of his lonely, depraved state; sweet to know he'd crossed the bridge to Christ.

It was also an answer to prayer.

For years now I had hoped, prayed, and fasted on his behalf. I had even asked Father for the special privilege of knowing this side of heaven if Nick found his way to Him. Now my heart was filled with gratitude that God had allowed me the gift of, through prayer, participating in His plan for Nick's redemption.

In 1 Thessalonians 5:17 we are told to pray without ceasing. In Luke 18:1 we learn that Jesus told his disciples a parable of a widow who persistently petitioned a judge for help "to show that at all times they ought to pray and not to lose heart." Prayer matters more than we will ever understand this side of heaven.

I tried to see Nick twice when I went to visit family in Phoenix, but neither time worked out for him. I was disappointed but knew that God had done a marvelous work.

In the meantime, Brad and I continued growing and learning alongside our friends and children. One year, Kathy and I went with our youth group on a mission trip to Ecuador. Jake and Ali went too. As we watched them share the message of Christ, loving on others with practical acts of kindness, I thought about one of Jake's first questions about Jesus. I think he was three or four when he asked, "If God is real, why can't we see Him?"

Now I found Him everywhere I looked.

Jake eventually returned to Ecuador after high school for a mission program before college. Jessie and Anna were becoming more independent as well.

Life was changing.

Pastor Steve was always saying "Living things grow, and growing things change."

I sensed change in our futures. Time and time again I found myself mulling over the phrase, "Follow Me and obey." Follow Him? Sure thing! But where?

I remembered the verse found in Deuteronomy: "Be strong and courageous, do not be afraid or tremble . . . for the LORD your God is the one who goes with you. He will not fail you or forsake you" (31:6).

I hung on to those words.

THE LETTER

I loved my role at the church. I loved the people. There were always more people. The more we grew as a church, the busier Brad and I became. I didn't want to miss out on any part, and often overextended my schedule until I was too busy, but it was for God, so that made it okay, right?

Without realizing it, I had begun to prioritize the *things* of God over time with Him and with my family.

One morning I was in the Word when I felt inspired to write myself a note that read, *Write Nick.*

I didn't know what I was supposed to write, but I knew it was Father giving me something He wanted me to do. I'd grown accustomed to His voice, so it wasn't a question of *if* I'd heard from Him. I knew this was from Him.

I put the neon green sticky note on my desk in clear view so I wouldn't forget it. I had a busy day, but I would get to it later.

Fast-forward eight and a half months. Every New Year we participated in a church-wide fast. One evening toward the end of the fast, I was exhausted. My body was weak from fasting. I decided to turn in early.

Brad and the girls were watching a movie. I kissed Brad good night. "I'm gonna take a few minutes alone, then go to bed." I went into my prayer closet, which I had equipped with my desk, a Bible, and a computer. I turned on some music. As I was singing, "Abba, I Belong to You," I became aware of His presence.

The song ended, but I didn't want to leave that special time with Father.

I told Him, "Okay, Lord, forget the sleep. I need YOU. What can I give You right now? What can I give to You that you don't already have?"

Even as I asked the question, my eyes were drawn to the little green sticky note.

"Write Nick."

It had been on my desk for over eight months. I knew He wanted me to write to Nick when I wrote the words on the paper. In fact, I had picked up the note numerous times, cleaning my desk or shuffling papers around, knowing better than to throw it away.

I had been telling myself that everything with Nick was complete, so why bother to write him a note? We'd even spoken briefly a couple of times since he contacted Mom with news that he had reconciled with God. He was in my prayers daily. What more could there be? What could I possibly say to him at this point?

I held the sticky note as His words washed over me, *"There's always more."*

Feeling convicted, I began to pray. "Over eight months. Wow. I am sorry, Lord. I've been following my own agenda, putting my plans over Yours." As I spoke the words, I realized this had become habitual.

The Great I AM watched his daughter's tears fall on the note. "Have you become too busy for Me?" he asked tenderly.

He reflected on the fact that every time His busy children woke up from their distractedness, they would open their eyes—and be surprised to find Him right before them.

"I never leave, child. I am always here. Now . . . write Nick."

I opened my computer in obedience. Tears spilled as I realized, again, how the ugliness of me had crept in.

Even so, the Lord's sweet presence filled me with peace. I didn't have a clue what to write. Everything had been said that I could possibly think to say. So that's what I typed. "Nick, I don't know what to write, but. . ."

As soon as I began, thoughts and words poured through my fingertips and onto my screen.

The message was all about God's perspective of Nick. How He sees Nick. He gave me *His* insight on events in Nick's life as well as His view on some positive character traits of Nick's that I would not have recognized on my own. It was thrilling. This was a love letter from the King, and I was being used as His messenger.

"Oh, Lord!" I cried out. "I can't wait for him to read this. It's going to make him laugh and cry. It will touch deeply into his heart. Awww! Why didn't I do this sooner, when You first asked?"

In the morning, I told Mom what happened, then asked, "Do you have Nick's current address?"

She said she didn't but promised to check with one of his relatives and get it for me.

I was so excited. I thought, *Wow, God. He's gonna love this.*

Nick would be so encouraged to read words that only Father would know to tell him.

Mom came by later that evening. We were in the kitchen when she said, "Shelly, I was able to get Nick's address."

"Sweet!" I had the letter stamped and ready to go. It just needed the address. "Let me get the envelope." I started to walk into the other room.

"Shelly."

I stopped and turned around.

Mom took a long, slow breath. "Shelly, Nick passed away two days ago."

I couldn't believe the words.

"Two days," I repeated slowly, my brain trying to process what I'd just heard. Suddenly I cried aloud, "But Lord, *why? You knew!*"

Immediately, two scriptures flooded my thoughts, the first one 1 Samuel 15:22: "But Samuel replied, 'What is more pleasing to the LORD: your burnt offerings and sacrifices or your obedience to his voice?' Listen! Obedience is better than sacrifice, and submission is better than offering the fat of rams" (NLT).

The second was Romans 11:29: "For the gifts and the calling of God are irrevocable."

God gifted me the blessing of being a messenger to Nick. He didn't revoke it because of my disobedience—or because Nick was in heaven.

How many times had Brad and I told our own kids, "Delayed obedience is disobedience"?

The letter was no use to Nick now. He was with Jesus when I wrote it. Yet, God didn't withhold from me the beautiful experience of obeying Him and writing down His thoughts to Nick.

Neither did He condemn me or shame me—but I felt I had totally missed an amazing opportunity.

Nick's undelivered letter was a wake-up call.

I thought of John 10:27, where Jesus says "My sheep hear My voice, and I know them, and they follow Me." What else had I missed out on by not following Jesus when He spoke to me?

I felt a gentle redirection in my spirit. *"Child, I'm not interested in what you can do for Me. I want you to do things with Me. Spend time with Me and I will tell you great things which you don't know."*

I began to streamline my daily schedule, adding more time alone with the King.

He led and I followed. Every day, I had a new question for Him: "Who do You want me to reach out to today, Lord?"

Or: "I have a really busy day. What do I need to know?"

Or perhaps: "I have a free day, Lord. How should I spend it?"

And sometimes: "Lord, that person could really use help. What would You like me to do?

But the privilege wasn't *doing things for Him* as much as it was *spending time with Him*. I continued to meet with Father, always asking: "What do You want, Father?"

For months, I felt the answer in my heart: *"Child, I want you. I want your attention. I want your affection."*

And then one day the answer changed: *"It's time. Let's begin."*

Begin? I didn't understand.

A verse from Isaiah came to mind: "Behold, I will do something new, now it will spring forth; will you not be aware of it? I will even make a roadway in the wilderness, rivers in the desert" (43:19).

I'd known in my spirit that change was coming. I had been feeling it—and ignoring it—for some time.

"I'm taking you someplace new. Follow Me. Tell your story."

Brad and I knew we were coming close to the end of an amazing season in our church community and in our lives. I still didn't know what God had in store for us, but at least I knew now that writing my story was going to be part of it.

Problem was, I didn't have a clue how to begin.

SOMETHING NEW

a new season was on the horizon. Brad and I were on our knees. I prayed, "Lord, what will it look like?"

"Follow Me. Tell your story."

For months I would wake up and spend precious time with the King. While that time was rich, I also felt as if I were walking in the dark, not knowing which direction to go. I began writing down some of my memories, but there was still much I needed to understand about what the Lord had in mind for us.

On March 4, 2014, I woke up and before my feet even hit the floor I knew.

"Today's the day, child. Follow Me."

I knew He was talking about my role on staff.

I asked Brad for prayer and a blessing. Our pastor friend, Eric, was in town and staying with us. He joined our prayer and then chuckled. "You do know what today is, right?"

No. Did I miss an important date?

I thought hard. "Umm . . . St. Patty's Day?"

Eric smiled. "No, it's March 4."

I still didn't get it.

He smiled again. "Shelly, today is March *fourth*. You are *marching forth*."

March forth, March 4. This day would radically change the direction of my life.

Later that morning I *marched forth* to ask Pastor Steve's and Pastor Dustin's blessing as I gave notice to step out of my role on staff. I had the utmost respect for these men, and their blessing was important to me. I literally was shaking as I asked to meet with them.

I sat down at the familiar table where as a staff we'd met for prayer or brainstorming so many times over the years. I felt like a kid asking for a blessing to leave home and go off to serve in another land—and I didn't even know anything about that other land.

The church was our home—our family. I loved being part of what the King was doing here. I loved the staff and our people. To top that, the growth we'd prayed, sown, and labored toward was beginning to take off; the harvest was ripe.

I felt as though I would miss out on so much. I remember praying, "Lord, will You keep me from reaping all that we've labored to plant and tend here?"

"The harvest is Mine, child."

I had known this day would come. Father had been preparing my heart for well over a year. But taking action to end one profound season of my life—without the excitement of knowing what the next season was going to hold—simply served to emphasize the ending. It felt so final.

"Faith, child. Without it, it's impossible to please Me. You know this. Now walk it out."

"Yes, Lord."

Brad and I would walk it out together. Letting go of the role I loved dearly felt like I was taking a step backward, but to not take the step would have been disobedience. It would have been like running backwards.

I remembered the hikes Dad took us on as kids. "We thought we were going to the top of the mountain," we'd say.

"We are."

"But Dad, we're going in the opposite direction."

Dad would press on with the words "You'll see." We'd plug along, sometimes with the mountain behind us, yet eventually, we'd arrive at the crest of the mountain.

Often, the best route up a mountain is by way of switchbacks. When the mountain is steep, the optimal path may actually take you at times in the opposite direction of your desired destination. It may appear that you are going the wrong way, but in truth you are advancing on the best possible route. Stepping out of my role on staff felt like a switchback.

I took a deep breath and reminded myself of the Scripture "Trust in the LORD with all your heart and do not lean on your own understanding. In all your ways acknowledge Him and He will make your paths straight" (Proverb 3:5–7).

Soon after that, I was offered a position with Caring Transitions, a company specializing in estate sales and helping seniors downsize and relocate. The King continued preparing Brad and me for our next assignment.

Throughout the following months, Brad and I spent a lot of time on our knees. As we focused on the King, the details of our next assignment became clear. We would move to Colorado, where Jake had settled. We would buy our own Caring Transitions franchise. Something about serving people through difficult transitions felt right.

Once the details became clear, the clock seemed to speed into overdrive. Everything began to happen quickly. Again, I had to fight for time alone with Father, but I needed it more than ever.

Martin Luther nailed it when he said he was too busy *not* to pray.

A little over a year after marching forth and stepping out of my church role, Brad and I sold our big, beautiful home and much of what we owned. We began the process of starting our own business in Colorado.

In late spring a houseful of friends helped us pack our remaining belongings, then load the moving truck.

Kathy was there the whole weekend. She had been there when we moved into our first home. Now she was with us as we prepared to leave our last home in Texas. It was bittersweet.

Saying goodbye to our people was the hardest thing to do. We said goodbye to Kathy, our church family, other friends, *our lives.*

It was hardest to say goodbye to two loved ones in particular. The first was Jessie. She would not be going with us.

"Mom, I have to stay here," she told me. "I want to do a second-year internship." She would stay with friends to finish an internship at our church. I understood this was an essential time and place of growth for her. I was certain Father was telling me, *"I've got her. Remember: she's Mine."*

My mom, too, would stay in Texas. "Shelly, I'm not ready to make such a big move," she explained.

It was a tough season preparing to let go.

I saw Mom one more time and gave a last hug. "I hope you'll consider catching up with us later in Colorado, Mom."

Gazing at her, I thought about how far we had come. I prayed, "God, this parting is so different from that day at Six Flags so long ago. Please take care of her until we can be together again."

After an exhausting weekend of clearing the house, packing our belongings, loading the truck, and saying goodbye, we spent our last night in Texas at a friend's home. Jessie spent the night with us there. Brad and I would leave before dawn the next morning.

It was late when we finally were able to clean up and get ready for bed.

"Mom. Do you have any conditioner?" Jessie asked.

"Sorry, doll. It's in a suitcase underneath a pile of coats in the car. Want me to get it? Or I can ask Miss Sue."

Our friends David and Sue had already gone to bed. Brad was already asleep as well.

Jessie shook her head. "No, Mom. That's fine. Thanks."

I knew she wanted to be done so she could catch some sleep. She'd worked tirelessly all weekend and had to be at work early in the morning.

God, this is my last time with Jessie.

I waited for her to wash her hair. Gratefully, she let me brush and dry her hair after she'd showered. I hadn't done that in years.

We hadn't found conditioner, and the shampoo seemed to have left a sticky residue. It was stiff and unrelenting to the brush. I had to hold back tears and laughter as I tried to detangle it.

Oh, God, I am beyond exhausted here. Help!

I started to laugh.

Jesus, help.

Sitting there with Jess, brushing her hair, I had begun to relax. I was afraid that if I continued laughing, I would lose it and end up in sobs.

God, I don't want to say goodbye. This is so difficult!

I managed to pull it together. After finishing her hair, I prayed over Jessie and all that lay ahead for her in the year to come. We said good night and would say goodbye in the morning.

Finally, I laid my head down for the night.

Jesus, this hurts so bad.

I fell asleep with a mix of tears and prayers.

The next morning, it was still dark when Brad hooked up the trailer. Then he said, "We're good to go."

Jessie gave us final hugs and waved at the curb. The physical ache of goodbye had already set in.

Once we were out of the city, a light mist of rain enshrouded us, diminishing our view. It mirrored our limited visibility of what lay ahead of us. We didn't say anything, silently processing thoughts and tears.

The rain ebbed over several hours until we neared the Texas border. Texas had been home, a good home, for twenty-two years. It was where we came to life in Christ; where we grew and raised a family. The clouds darkened as we crossed the state line. Brad looked at me, sweetly attempting to provoke a smile. My tears broke loose again.

I remembered the Bible passage, "Go therefore . . . and lo, I am with you always, even to the end of the age" (Matthew 28:19–20). He calls us to go and assures us He will be with us. The purpose is always the kingdom. I knew that, but still, my soul warred within.

We crossed the New Mexico border into Colorado as the truck chugged up the Raton Pass. Everything we'd acquired in the last two decades was either being hauled up the mountain or had been sold to prepare for whatever we were being called to do next.

Jake and Anna were waiting for us in Colorado Springs. Jake had been living there for a year and teaching at a Christian school. Anna had moved there recently to enroll in the same school and begin classes. We would crash at Jake's bachelor pad for a month until the townhome we'd rented came available.

I was familiar with the comforting words in Matthew 28:20: "I am with you always." Now I thought of them constantly, hearing them spoken in the loving voice of Father.

Putting action to a dream reveals the extent to which our souls are surrendered to the King. It was more difficult than I expected. I had to take my thoughts captive not just by the hour but by the minute. Countless questions went off like popcorn in my mind:

God, did we hear You clearly? (Brad and I were united, agreeing that we had). *What grocery store will we go to? When will our bodies adjust to the altitude? Who will I meet for pie? Will our business take off?*

And the hardest question of all: *God, why does this feel so awful?*

We couldn't stop and go backward, but forward hurt. It was costly.

I felt stripped of so many good things.

We were in a new city in a new state. Our children were the only people we knew. We had no church. No community. We no longer had the safe haven of our own home or our own belongings. *Are we crazy?*

The invisible God was with us, prodding us forward into a new land. Once again, I thought about God's words to Joshua as He sent him forward into new territory: "Have I not commanded you? Be strong and courageous! Do not tremble or be dismayed, for the LORD your God is with you wherever you go" (Joshua 1:9). I'd sure needed those words a lot lately. I needed to be strong and courageous too. I needed to remember that we were not alone—that we had never been alone—and that the Lord was with us every step of the way.

We looked for a church right away. I could hear Pastor Steve saying, "Get with God's people." We began searching.

I expected to find a church just like the Harvest, but with a different name and faces—but nothing felt like home. It was awkward walking into crowds of people as strangers.

Every Sunday I silently prayed, *Lord, we don't know anybody. Will this ever feel like home?*

Not to mention that the culture of Colorado Springs is radically different from the refinement and extravagance of the Dallas metroplex or even the polished eclectic mix of LA.

In our first month here, in the heart of old Colorado City, we saw more tattoos per square inch of skin, and more purple, green, and blue hair, than I'd seen in my entire life to that point.

Father, surely You don't want us here. We are so out of place, it isn't even funny.

Finally, we had no income and no backup stash—only a new business and no community to network within.

This wasn't about us though.

God reminded me, *"You are not here for you, but for Me and My kingdom. There's more, child. Watch and see. You are Mine. I have led you here for a reason. Yes, I'm stripping you down. I want you fully dependent on Me. And, child, look around you."*

And so I did.

Here we were surrounded by the majestic beauty of the Colorado Rockies, pine trees, creeks, and countless trails to explore.

In all my years of running, I had never done any serious trail runs. I began to escape into the pines and boulders for amazing times with the Lord. The beauty of His creation echoed His magnificence. As I ran, I often thought of this verse: "He made the earth by his power; he founded the world by His wisdom and stretched out the heavens by his understanding." (Jeremiah 51:15 NIV)

Sometimes, as I looked at Pike's Peak, massive in the near distance, it dawned on me that writing my story and starting a business seemed as insurmountable as that peak. And there were other challenges too.

One day Brad and I climbed the Incline at the base of the Pike's Peak. It's just a small portion of the mountain itself—just under a mile. But because it's a direct ascent at about a 60 percent incline, the climb is daunting, steep, dangerous, and scary. It's both exciting and challenging.

The climb seemed to reflect everything Brad and I were facing together. Not just the move and starting a new business, but also in our marriage. The move had been hard on our relationship but, like going up the Incline, there was no turning back. We had finished an incredible season growing and raising our children as we became fortified in Christ. Now it was time to apply everything we had learned and become to something brand-new. God had invited us to join Him on a daring new adventure.

"This is ridiculous," I panted as we crawled slowly upward. The height set my head reeling and legs shaking.

Brad and I struggled step after step. But we did it. And we did it together.

Slowly our business grew. The Lord brought us like-minded people with whom to begin to build a team. And when we weren't spending time with God, enjoying our precious children, or building a business caring for others, I wrote. Whenever I could find spare moments in our busy days, I was being obedient and writing my story.

God had stirred us up and called us out. He was not stripping us down to punish us; He was refining and cleansing us. Once we were in Colorado and I had the benefit of hindsight, I realized that before the move, I'd become comfortable. Pride had sprouted up in my heart, and I had become more satisfied with the approval of my peers than with the approval of my Father.

The King is always there, always present, but He doesn't coddle.

One day Anna and I decided to try to climb the whole of Pike's Peak. We wanted to ascend our first fourteener together. As a runner, I considered myself fit. We chose the back side, which is a steeper, more direct ascent. I optimistically exclaimed, "We can do this, Anna!"

We knew it would be a full-day excursion, but we had no idea how difficult it would be. By the time we made it to tree line, I was already spent—and we had farther to go!

At one point we paused and noticed that there weren't many people on the path. Still, we felt compelled to continue. The switchbacks lessened and the grade increased. We looked at each other and pressed on. I was grateful to be up there with my Anna.

As we climbed higher, the air became noticeably thinner. Hiking at twelve thousand feet, you become aware of all the muscles throughout your body; they all cry out for oxygen.

Before our final ascent, the steepest portion, I thought I might go into cardiac arrest.

I could feel my pulse pounding in my skull.

"Anna, I don't think I can finish," I said weakly. I looked below and my head swam.

Anna pressed on, "Mom, we can do this!"

Lord, I can't let her down. What kind of example am I setting here?

I looked at my swollen fingers. My wedding ring was tight.

But dear God, help. There's no air up here.

Clouds were thickening nearby. We needed to reach the summit and then descend back below tree line to be out of danger in case lightning started. Once again fear was at my heels.

Pike's Peak is one of America's top ten most dangerous mountains to climb because of its form and placement at the forefront of the Rockies. There is an area just below the final ascent known as Devil's Playground. It's the perfect arrangement for summer afternoon lightning storms. The peak attracts electricity and the Playground is littered with scattered boulders on which lightning strikes and bounces onto others.

I hated that fear had caught up to me here on the side of the mountain. It loomed close like the clouds thickening around us; fearful thoughts of "what if" at every step threatened to paralyze me as I looked down the steep drops.

I was reminded to take every thought captive.

It dawned on me that if the Lord could get me to the top of that seemingly impossible mountain, surely He would help me summit the other mountains in my life.

I thought of all the other insurmountable challenges He had helped me overcome over the years—even when I couldn't see Him.

Even when all I could see were obstacles and pain.

Even when I couldn't begin to imagine seeing myself or my circumstances from His perspective.

From His vast and eternal vantage point, the King looked down on the Peak.

The shadow of His magnificent presence fell on the mountain.

The shadow of His presence fell on the woman and the girl, both His daughters—and with his presence came grace.

The shadow of His presence fell on everything.

He'd always been there, strong and stable, unchanging and unshakable, timeless.

I took a big breath and looked at Anna proceeding fearlessly. Sometimes you just have to kick fear in the face and move on.

We climbed on and made our way to the top. Carefully, I braced myself on a boulder and surveyed the spectacular view. It was amazing. It was steep and rugged but beautiful.

"Wow, Anna. We did it."

From here we could see everything.

EPILOGUE

*W*riting the final words of the final chapter, I knew that my book might be finished, but my story was not. In order to share it with others, I needed the blessing of those whose lives and stories were entwined with mine.

Brad gave me his full support from the first to last page. He selflessly encouraged me to include even the dark, dirty, nitty-gritty aspects of our relationship. As he says, how do we celebrate the magnitude of God's grace if we can't acknowledge the depths from which He redeems us?

My experience climbing Pike's Peak taught me another lesson: Every mountaintop experience comes with some kind of descent, and that can be scary. When you descend, you have to look down the whole way. You are not face-to-face, clinging to the mountain; you must face outward, openly exposed.

I felt as if writing my story was like climbing the mountain. When it was done, I had an exceptional view of just how far we had come, how much ground we had traveled with the Lord in this journey of life. Seeing my life from His perspective was exhilarating and life changing in every way!

Sharing my story with my family was very much like making the steep climb downward. I had not considered risk coming down. I felt exposed. Would I stumble and fall down on the descent? Would I hurt others in the process?

After Brad, Dad would be the first to read my story. I was tempted to take out one chapter, then another. It would be hard for him to read. It would also be hard for him to know that other people would learn of our wounds and failings. Would telling my story—all of it—cost me my relationship with my dad? It had taken decades to be restored. Could I risk losing it again?

I sat down at my computer to slice, dice, and chop out the painful parts. As my fingers touched the keys, Father's voice surrounded me in a tender whisper, *"There are no shortcuts on My mountain, love."*

I prayed, "Lord, this will hurt. I don't want to awaken pain in anyone. I can't bear to lose Dad again or anyone else . . . not at the work of my hands or heart. And what about Mom? She has carried her own regrets all these years. How will she handle the weightiness of this?"

Is this not My assignment to you? I have called you to this. Would you withhold the whole of it from Me? Trust me, child. Follow Me . . . whatever it costs."

Dad and Miss Ellie came to visit on the weekend of the one-year anniversary of our move to Colorado Springs. We had a wonderful time together. Toward the end of their time with us, I gave Dad my manuscript. I had made the difficult decision to keep it as it was, without deleting anything I had written.

"Dad, I want you to read this. This is my story. It's our story."

He and Miss Ellie graciously accepted the manuscript. All I could do was hold on to hope, trusting Father for their hearts to be protected.

Soon after they left, I spoke with Dad. He'd read it. He owned it with grace, dignity, and humility, giving me his blessing. God's grace had anchored our relationship.

Mom read it, too, with a broken heart. Then she graciously encouraged me to continue with the telling of God's redemptive work in all of our lives.

Our stories are evidence of the Father's glory, revealed in the lives of His children. Our stories have power.

I began my story with the following thoughts, and I feel them so strongly that I must close with them as well . . .

Where is Jesus in *your* story?

My greatest desire is that my story will stir in you an awareness of His presence in your own life—even when you haven't sensed Him there.

Because He *has* been there. Every step of the way. You are not invisible to Him, *and you never have been*. He sees you. Embracing this truth —and understanding the loving, protective, redemptive way He sees you—will transform your story and your life. Are you ready for beautiful memories to be made even richer? Are you willing for painful memories to be redeemed, and to discover meaning and treasure waiting for you even there?

Then what are you waiting for? Ask Him to empower you to see Him clearly in your own story, past, present, and all that is yet to come.

HAVE YOU MET JESUS?

If you have yet to welcome Jesus into your heart and your story, there's no better time than now! Make these your heartfelt words to Him:

> *Jesus, something in my life isn't working. I need hope and healing and even a miracle or two, and the Bible says that You're the source of all these good things.*

> *I understand that You are God's Son, and that You died on the cross to pay for my sins, then rose again so that I can have eternal life with You. Your Word promises me that you have good plans for my life.*

> *I want all of these things, Jesus. I want everything you have for me. Please forgive my sins, make me your own, and write my name in Your Book of Life!*

> *Thank You, Jesus. I belong to You now. Please show me what it means to follow You.*

If you prayed this prayer, here are some next steps:

- Tell someone who knows Jesus about your prayer today.
- Ask Jesus to show you where you can find encouragement and fellowship with other Christ-followers.
- Open a Bible and invite the Holy Spirit to speak to you as you read God's love letters to you.

And please email me at shelly@shellybusby.com and let me know so I can celebrate with you and pray for you!

CONNECT WITH SHELLY

Shelly has shared with you how she came to see Jesus in her own story. Learning to see and appreciate God's involvement in our lives—past, current, and present—is an ongoing process. There are always new insights to embrace as we continue growing in Christ and inviting the Holy Spirit into unexplored terrain in our very souls.

What an intimate, precious, and lifelong journey it is!

Would you love some company and encouragement along the way?

If so, Shelly would love to hear from you.

Connect through her website and social media for more encouraging words from Shelly, and you'll also have opportunities to share your own story.

Visit **www.shellybusby.com** to:

- Connect with Shelly on social media
- Discover more resources that will leave you encouraged and equipped

- Learn about opportunities to share insights from your own journey
- Share relevant blog posts and content with your friends
- Find out how to invite Shelly to speak to women in your church or community

Blessings to you on your journey!

ABOUT THE AUTHOR

Shelly Busby is passionate about helping women find freedom from the lies and hurts that are holding them back—including finding freedom from the deep wounds that come from sexual abuse. Formerly Director of Adult Ministries at The Harvest (now Church Eleven 32) in Allen, Texas, today Shelly shares her message of hope with women around the country. She lives with her husband, Brad, in Colorado Springs, Colorado.

For information on how you can invite Shelly to speak to women in your church or community:

Email events@shellybusby.com

Visit www.shellybusby.com

CPSIA information can be obtained
at www.ICGtesting.com
Printed in the USA
FFHW020621240219
50647960-56060FF